Divine Grace

Lorna Bogues

Messianic & Christian Publisher

Published by
Olive Press צהר זית
Messianic and Christian Publisher
P.O. Box 567
Port Leyden, NY 13433
and
1326 N. Winton Rd.
Rochester, NY

www.olivepresspublisher.org

Our prayer at Olive Press is that we may help make the Word of Adonai fully known, that it spread rapidly and be glorified everywhere. May our books help open people's eyes so they will turn from darkness to Light and from the power of the adversary to God and to trust in ישוע Yeshua (Jesus).
(From II Thess. 3:1; Col. 1:25; Acts 26:18,15 NRSV and CJB, the *Complete Jewish Bible*)

Cover and interior design by Cheryl Zehr, Olive Press
Front cover photo by Cheryl Zehr

Printed in the USA
ISBN 978-0-9790873-4-9
1. Christian Parenting 2. Parenting Teens 3. Inspirational

DEFIANT DAUGHTER *Divine Grace*
Copyright © 2009 by Lorna Bogues.
All rights reserved No part of this book may be reproduced, stored in a retrieval system or transmitted in any way by any means—electronic, mechanical, photocopy, recording or otherwise—without the prior permission of the copyright holder, except as provided by USA copyright law.

All scripture quotations unless otherwise noted are taken from the *Holy Bible, New International Version* (NIV). Copyright © 1973, 1978, 1984 by International Bible Society. All rights reserved.

Scriptures marked:

- KJV are taken from the *King James Version*. Public domain.
- NKJV are taken from the *New King James Version*. Copyright © 1982 by Thomas Nelson, Inc. All rights reserved.
- NCV are taken from the New Century Version. Copyright 1987, 1988, 1991 by Word Publishing, a division of Thomas Nelson, Inc. Used by permission. All rights reserved.

In honor to God, pronouns referring to the Trinity are capitalized.

It gives me the deepest pleasure to dedicate this book to my daughter, Candi.

Trials are never welcome, but God has shown Himself faithful to Candi and me. He has used these recordings to bring glory and honor to His Name. Our walk with Him has been strengthened. I pray that this, our memoir, will touch hearts and win souls for our one and only Lord and Savior, the Man Christ Jesus, our Jewish Messiah, Yeshua.

Foreword

So many of us look forward to becoming a parent. The rewards touch our hearts to its very depth; the love is so great. There is none like it. But the dichotomy of this relationship is the depth of the hurt it also brings: Hurting because your child is hurting; hurting because your child is not heading in the right direction in life. This is something else again, when you are a Christian and, though you've taught your child the things of God, he/she is not walking in obedience to you or to God.

Lorna and I had so many heart-to-heart talks over the years as we walked along the Erie Canal in Rochester. We spilled our hearts out with love and concern for our children and ended with prayer for them. During those times, as Lorna shared her struggles with Candi, I listened and pondered. Many times my response was just, "Oh dear." I could understand Lorna's frustrations, but I must admit, there were times when I felt she was too tough on Candi. (In my interactions with Candi, she was just such a sweet, young woman.) Though I disagreed with Lorna a number of times and she knew it, it never put a damper on our friendship. Truly a blessing from God!

As the years have gone on, Lorna has remained steadfast in the Lord and in her expectations of Candi. There were many tough times. Now, as Lorna and I continue to walk and chat, I hear her express gratitude to God for the fine young woman Candi has become. Candi and her mom have a truly loving relationship and Christ is a very important part of it. Candi knows where her mother stands—on Jesus, her Rock!

Jean Hink

Table of Contents

Foreword

Introduction

Chapter 1	Where's My Sweet Daughter?	9
Chapter 2	Unbearable Tension	27
Chapter 3	Will Counseling Help?	41
Chapter 4	My Little Girl is Back!!	59
Chapter 5	Orange Peels and Basketball Boy	67
Chapter 6	Almost to the Breaking Point	81
Chapter 7	Jealousy Triangle and a Blue Car	91
Chapter 8	Music and Earrings	101
Chapter 9	Nice Surprises	111
Chapter 10	Candi as an Adult	129
Chapter 11	The Lord is Good	135

Editor's note:

   Lorna is a cheerful, friendly person. I love being around her because my spirits are always lifted. I also love her endearing accent and manner of speaking. Growing up in Jamaica, she was given basically a British education. As you read this book, please enjoy the bit of British flavor in the way Lorna crafts some of her sentences.

Introduction

I am writing this little book because, for the first year after my husband left, I kept a journal which has been significant in ultimately shaping who my daughter, Candi, is today. I gave it to her as a little memoir the day she left home to start college in 1998. Candi has since shared the journal with many friends. I did not want to lose it, so I decided to write a little book and share it instead. In so doing, Candi and I will always have my original journal as a testimony of God's faithfulness during a very difficult period in our lives.

I am very much against divorce. Allow me to reiterate. In no way do I want to be promoting single parenting. It is NOT God's ideal. He made Adam and Eve, the first parents, a male and a female. Therefore, I believe that is the model He desires for us, but as you will see later, I really had no other choice.

In 1996 when my husband and I were divorced, I encountered a variety of changes, very different from anything I could ever have anticipated. The experiences were quite significant and through them I have learned a lot. Most of these occurrences have played themselves out through Candi, causing her to become most unapproachable, disagreeable, and incorrigible. This journal is a bird's-eye view of that very difficult period in my daughter's and my life.

Before I set the tone for telling exactly how this journal came about, I want to emphasize that our walk with Christ is a personal one. He speaks to all of us differently and does not necessarily require the same things from each of us. What worked for me may not necessarily be applicable for someone else, but one thing is absolutely sure, God is the same yesterday, today, and forever. He will never abandon us as orphans.

God will never leave us nor forsake us and in the time of our greatest need, He does His greatest work. He is faithful, patient, loving, forgiving, and longsuffering. Now, those are not all of His attributes, but they are certainly the ones that were most powerful and prevalent in my greatest hour of need.

Chapter One

WHERE'S MY SWEET DAUGHTER?

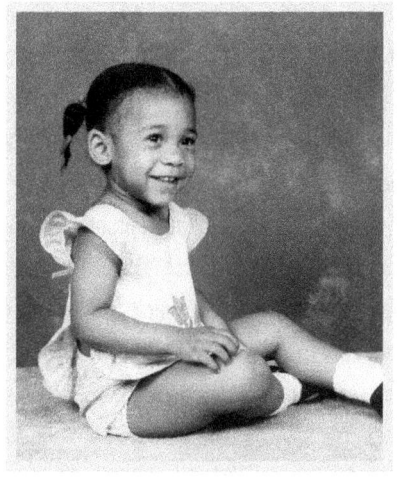

Candi age 18 months

Defiant Daughter *Divine Grace*

My fifteen-year-old daughter was a very sweet girl. She and I had a delightful, close relationship. Let me try and draw you a picture of what she was like. We both went to Church and did what most God-fearing committed Christians did. I had a personal relationship with Christ and, although Candi had not openly declared her faith through baptism, I believe that she did accept Christ as her Savior. You could always catch her living according to the tenets of the Christian faith.

She had a pet rabbit, Benji, that she always cared for well. She frequently took him out of his cage to play with him, often pulling a string around that he would chase after. Whenever she took him out, she would set up his poopy corner because he was paper trained. Her bedroom was never immaculate, unless she was planning to have friends over, but it was also never filthy. NEVER, did she leave her clothes on the floor. However, she rarely made her bed. She got $1 per day for each day that she made it. I think the most she ever earned was $15, usually when she knew that something was coming up like going skating or miniature golfing where she had to pay. She practiced her piano regularly, even choosing songs to practice ahead of time, so that whenever she was asked to play during the offertory at church, she would be prepared.

Her father never went to church, but one day he said he would join us. It was 1992. He and I had some problems in our relationship, and he thought that if the family worshipped together, it would improve our life. Candi, then age eleven, was elated and quite ecstatic. Since we had both been praying for him, it seemed reasonable to believe that the Lord was answering our prayers.

My husband came to church for a few Sundays and many congregants, as Candi and I did, thought he had really changed. But then one day he announced that the services were boring, and he was going to visit other churches. When he found the right one, we could all change and worship as a family. I agreed. Well, a few weeks later, he came back and said that he had found the ideal one: Kingdom Hall of Jehovah's Witnesses. At that time, I didn't really know much about this group, except that they knocked on your door on Saturday mornings and left you a *Watchtower*. However, the Ruach HaKodesh (Hebrew for "Holy Spirit") is alive and well, and I immediately got a check in my spirit. I did some research and found out that Jehovah's Witnesses is a cult. I informed my husband that I wouldn't go to their assembly. He reminded me that both Candi and I were supposed to accompany him because that was the agreement. I refused, but Candi decided to go with him. I really didn't want her to, but I believe that the Ruakh HaKodesh (Holy Spirit) prevented me from causing a scene. Well, lo and behold, Candi came back home and informed me that those people weren't Christians. I rest my case. Being only eleven years old, how could she know they weren't Christians? I am sure that this revelation came from our Heavenly Father. Out of the mouths of babes and sucklings, a truth revealed.

Well, my husband set to work to convert both Candi and me. In case you, the reader, have not yet figured it out, Satan and the Lord cannot coexist peacefully under the same roof, but that is what my husband was attempting. It didn't work. Suffice it to say, we were as close to Armageddon as I ever want to get.

During this time, Candi was most attentive and loving to me. Jehovah's Witnesses do not celebrate anything except wedding anniversaries. Candi saved her money to buy me flowers and gifts for Mother's Days and my birthdays. This really touched me.

I love Candi very much and as my only child, I protected and shielded her from a lot of things. But I was unable to protect her from what happened next. Since my husband was not getting anywhere in trying to encourage, convince, persuade, cajole, bribe me—whatever means he could conjure up—to get me to come his way, he turned his attention to our daughter. He figured that if he tried to make her life as miserable as possible, he would win us both over because I would do anything for Candi's happiness. Well, it didn't work, but it made our living together up to 1996 pure torture.

The worst incident came one quiet Saturday night. My husband and Candi were having a rare moment of relaxing father-daughter time. I was upstairs, when suddenly the stillness was shattered by Candi's piercing scream. I jumped up, but before I could even make it to the stairs, she rushed up the steps in record time and collapsed in my arms, sobbing uncontrollably. It was impossible to make any sense of what she was trying to say. I finally got her calm enough for her to explain.

Apparently, her dad took their time together to inform her that he did not want her to call him Dad anymore. His premise was that as an upstanding member of Kingdom Hall, on whom deaconship was going to be conferred, he represented morality and I represented immorality. Since she had chosen immorality over morality, she could no longer call him Dad. I prayed with Candi and then we read Psalms 27 together. When she became calmer and more relaxed, she went to her room to get ready for bed.

I took a deep breath and calmly walked downstairs, ignoring the pounding in my breast, which I believe was more from anger than any other emotion. When I got to the den, I turned the television off and faced my husband. I asked him to explain to me who Candi's dad was, because if he weren't, then I definitely needed to find the person that

I had committed this immoral act with. He rather smugly gave me some inane excuse about the man being the head of the house and what Jehovah said about the woman's role and a bunch of other things in which I had no interest and frankly didn't have any desire to listen to anyway.

When my husband completed his ramblings, I sat down at the computer and wrote a long letter to Dr. James Dobson of Focus on the Family in which I gave a little overview of our situation and asked for advice. I did this because the Lord has told us in His word that in the multitude of counsel, there is wisdom. Dr. Dobson, I felt, was the most accredited and respected Christian psychologist on family affairs. A Focus on the Family counselor later contacted me, and we spoke over the phone. He prayed with me and suggested that maybe a period of separation was what was needed to pull the family together. I agreed with him. I later discussed it with my daughter and she agreed.

When I presented the idea to my husband, he agreed at first. Later he said that he had discussed it with the elders at Kingdom Hall who said he couldn't move out because he was counseling others to stay together, and it would reflect badly on him to go against his own counsel. He could only agree to do it under one condition, if the court authorized him to do so. I told him I would take care of that. The very next day I called an attorney and started proceedings to realize this goal.

I need to pause here and explain that even though I got the advice from Focus on the Family, I did not take the decision lightly to separate from my husband. I had rejected the idea of a divorce, but in my prayer time, seeking the Lord, I was directed by the Ruakh HaKodesh (Holy Spirit) to 2 Corinthians 6:14-18 which is noted in my Bible as April 30, 1996. These verses admonish us not to be unequally yoked with unbelievers as there is no relationship with righteousness and wickedness or harmony between Christ and Belial. The most poignant part to these verses is where the Lord commands us to come out from among them and **He will be a Father to us** (emphasis, mine). I was so shocked when I read these verses that I wrote in the column of my Bible, "Does this apply to my husband and me?" I believe that I had walked out of God's perfect will in my youth (of which I will elaborate later); nevertheless, in His grace and mercy, He was granting me His permissive will to separate myself from this man who was rejecting Truth and becoming a leader of lies.

On the day that both my husband and I appeared before the judge, the latter informed my attorney that he couldn't move on the case unless I filed a deposition.

My attorney then explained to me that, by that, the judge meant that I had to file for divorce. He was quick to reassure me that the case would be left open for a year. He was sure that by the end of the year, my husband would have come to his senses, that we would undoubtedly reconcile and no further litigation would be necessary. This, of course, would secure the separation which I wanted. I agreed, went home, shared all this with Candi, and she was quite happy about it. We prayed and I felt positive that she understood why I was taking the stand I was. At that moment there was never any indication whatsoever that she was angry, upset, fearful, or had any misgivings about what was happening or was about to proceed henceforth. Frankly, I sensed that she felt relieved. Was I ever wrong!

(Candi's presence was never requested in court, of which I am glad. I think it was ordeal enough for her to lose her dad, and I would have vehemently objected had the judge asked for her to be in attendance.)

My husband moved out of the house on Wednesday, September 5, 1996, exactly fifteen years to the day that we had officially become husband and wife. My sweet daughter left for school that morning, her first day back for the new school year. It was also my first day back to school. I am a teacher.

Lest you have forgotten, let me remind you that my daughter, up to this time, had been a sweet, loving, compliant, and very even-keeled young lady. Prior to that time, we did have our little ups and downs, but nothing that some hugs and kisses and our prayer time couldn't mend. Well, Candi woke up the following morning and I was thrown for a loop. This new child, I didn't know. She was surly, rude, aggressive, and totally morose. In my usual loving way, I tried to find out what was the matter. In the most ill-tempered way, my overtures were met with, "Nothing." The more I pressed, the more disrespectful she became, so I let it go for the moment.

Did I just say for the moment? Let me explain. From that time on, that was the new Candi. Each day she became surlier and surlier. I began to feel guilty and angry. I cried out to the Lord daily and felt that He wasn't hearing me. I felt that if I didn't do something, I would probably end up hurting my child badly. I realize now that it was the Lord who told me to write a journal which you can now read. (It is basically left in its original, unedited form even though in my stress, my thoughts were sometimes scattered.)

Wednesday, October 16, 1996

Dear Candi,

    I have been meaning to start writing to you in a journal, but each time I go to the store, I forget, so I found this notebook and decided to start today.

    Firstly, let me start afresh and anew by apologizing for the situation that I have put you in—practically fatherless, but I will reiterate once more that when we disobey our heavenly Father, we suffer dire consequences. I never sought God first and as a result, I have to pay. In so doing, you also end up being the recipient of the ill.

    The only problem is, Candi, God has forgiven me. I have done more for you as your mother, than I could ever have done, even if I had made the right choices initially.

    Thank God, I have used my mistakes as forewarning for you. I know that you are hurting, but I was hoping that you would understand and be more supportive.

    I am glad I read Dr. Dobson's book, <u>Parenting Isn't for Cowards</u> that you brought home from the church library. I never dreamed that the part about the compliant child turned rebellious was talking to me in any way, but I guess it was.

    In 1987 when I bought you your piano it was with the understanding that you would play until you left for college because $3,000 was too large a sum to pay for a white elephant. Well, now you've decided to quit. Your chores have become quite burdensome and tedious. I made out a schedule to help to point you in the right direction and to jolt you just a little bit. You made your bed once and you practiced your piano for a record one minute.

I am always on your back about Benji (a rabbit) because my heart will not allow me to watch the poor thing die of starvation.

Ever since your father left, we have not prayed or read the Bible even once. Candi, God is my source, my strength and my supplier. Without Him, I wouldn't be able to stand and today, I would be flat on my face, now that your father is gone.

I know on November 27th you are going to be angry and disappointed, but I cannot in good conscience use the money that God has put me in charge of, to buy you a car or pay for lessons if you continue to act this way. When we go home to be with the Lord, He will say, "Welcome thou good and faithful servant," or "Depart from me I know you not." If we don't comply, we won't reap His blessings.

I tried so hard to talk to you, but it just turned into a horrible scene, so I decided to leave you alone. Instead, I am talking to you through this journal which I will hand to you, when the time comes.

Love,
Mom

Thursday, Oct. 17, 1996

Dear Candi,

    A few minutes ago, the phone rang. It was Auntie Marcia. I wish I could imitate in a letter the gruffness, disrespect and aggravation with which you hollered for me. You see, I was in the bathroom and didn't hear the phone.

    "MOM   PHONE," you yelled. Your voice is reminisce of your dad's. Do you remember how with sarcasm you would sneer?

    "Right, sure, Daddy loves you."

    You see, Candi, you learned a lot from both your parents and the Bible never lies: "Train up a child in the way he should go ..." As parents we modeled the behaviors and you copied them.

    Have you ever thought that although I knew that your father didn't love me, I treated him the best way God taught me? He taught me how to "love your enemies, do good to those that hate you and despitefully use you" (Luke 6:35).

    I know in my heart and in my conscience, I did well by your dad. I also know that you saw how his behavior and attitude changed the more he got into Kingdom Hall. Yet, in spite of everything, you persist in treating me with such disrespect. I could slap you and do all manner of punishments, but I will restrain myself.

    Satan is working in our lives and I know God has allowed him for a greater good. Of course, I can't tell you what it is now, but my Father loves me (us), and I am trusting Him for the greater good.

    I really don't like your attitude, but I am willing to wait

for you to come back to a right relationship. Remember, God allows us to make our own choices, but until we come back to walk with Him and serve Him, we will forever miss out on the joys of His blessings and rewards. I love you, Candi, but I love God more and He is now teaching me who I really am. I picked a promise (from the Promise Box) which said:

> When He hath tried me, I shall come forth as gold.
> Job 23:10 KJV

God has loved me this much that He gave you to me as well as your dad to subdue me and to bring me back to a right relationship with Him. You probably think that your dad was the worst thing that could have happened to me, but unless I had sought God first in my childhood, then your father is the best thing that could have happened to me and quite frankly for you too.

Friday, Oct. 18, 1996, 9:16 P.M.

Dear Candi,

I am lying here listening to the rain and thinking about the state of your room. You see, I just went down there to leave $12.00 for PSAT's. I bet you haven't cleaned that room in at least three weeks. Last night I reminded you to clean Benji's poopy corner and I had to remind you again this morning.

Then again you got righteously indignant when I told your grandmother that you had quit piano. You still haven't folded the clothes from last weekend. Are your chores being taken care of? Did you know that the Bible says that if a man does not work, he should not eat? (2 Timothy 3:10).

Maybe all these things are happening because you need to learn the value of hard work so you will scrimp, save and penny pinch, like I have, and buy your own car.

God is not allowing our situation to wax cold for nothing. I believe all this is happening for a reason. Well, you and I will just have to trust in the Lord to see the end result.

Saturday, Oct. 19, 1996, 9:58 P.M.

Dear Candi,

Today you left home at 7:30 to do your PSAT's. You came back home from Clarence at almost 6:00 p.m. The first thing you wanted to know was if you could go to Nick's party. I told you no and you slammed the door and later yelled, "PHONE," when Juana called. I said nothing.

Just a few minutes ago, you were complaining how sick you are. It's pouring outside. It has been pouring all day. You were in the rain most of the day. The primary reason why I said no you couldn't go to the party, of course, was the chores that weren't done, but for many other reasons as well: your sickness, your being away all day and most of all you didn't deserve to go.

Sunday, Oct. 20, 1996

Dear Candi,

 Today was quite a normal day. It was pretty much like some of the good old times we used to have.

 You didn't seem to be as angry and uptight as you seem to have habitually been lately. I did ask your gut feeling on your dad's and my separating, but you said you honestly couldn't answer as you weren't sure yourself.

 Last time I checked though, Benji had nothing in his bowl. I hope that after your lesson with Mr. Wray your Sunday school teacher, on Matthew 10:37-39, you realized that God loves you and He is really calling you. It's not by sheer coincidence that the very scripture I pointed out to you last night would be the same one that your Father pointed you to today. I am praying that you will come to realize that Satan is sifting you and if God has given him permission, it's because He wants you to be mature in Him and trust Him.

 I hope that your vacation away from the piano will not be forever.

         Love in Him,
         Mom

Monday, Oct. 21, 1996

Dear Candi,

Today you looked like death warmed over. You are really sick. While I was standing in your room, I was surveying the mess, but I was good. I didn't say anything. You see, the room was dirty before you got sick and so was the overflowing garbage in the bathroom.

Aren't you happy that God provided Pastor to take you to school today? I wonder how you will react when they ask you to play piano at church.

Tonight I wanted to ask you one question. What exactly do you want to do in this house? But, one, you were sick and two, I didn't feel like dealing with any more dissension.

Love in Him,
Mom

Tuesday, Oct. 22, 1996

Dear Candi,

It has been quite a few days and you seem to be more even-keeled. You really haven't had the pouting. Come to think of it, it has been only three days, but considering all that has been happening, it seems like an eternity.

I know that your dad's leaving has been hard, for you, but at least you can see that you both have a much better relationship. You can talk to him and he reciprocates by actually listening. Frankly, he has even been much more willing to listen to you than before.

Lastly, I can't help it going back to the chores. Nothing has been done: your room is still a mess, Benji is still stopping his breath because of the poopy corner, and the piano seems to be eternally silenced.

You used to spend each night reading something from the Bible, but you don't any more. Candi, I just don't know.

Well, these are just food for thought.

In Christ,
Mom

Wednesday, Oct. 23, 1996

FOR BETTER OR WORSE — LYNN JOHNSTON

Panel 1: "DON'T WORRY ABOUT ELIZABETH, EL. SHE'S GOING TO BE ALL RIGHT."
Panel 2: "SHE HAS SOME GOOD FRIENDS—AND SHE GETS ALONG WELL WITH HER TEACHERS."
Panel 3: "SHE'S COURTEOUS AND HELPFUL AND HONEST... SHE'S REALLY A NICE KID!" "I KNOW, CONNIE."
Panel 4: "BUT WHY CAN'T SHE BE LIKE THAT AT HOME!!"

FOR BETTER OR FOR WORSE ©1996, Lynn Johnston Productions. Dist. By Universal Uclick. Reprinted with permission. All rights reserved.

Dear Candi,

Today I read the above cartoon and it really summarizes a lot of my feelings and frustrations in trying to guide, direct, teach, show, model and even reprimand you at times.

I think you understand what I am driving at by reading this for yourself. I also hope that you understand when

I explain about the piano just sitting there gathering dust. I would hope for your sake that you will start playing soon. After all, you have less than two years and before you know it, time will have flown by.

> **What would you do to encourage the cooperation of my 15-year-old son who deliberately makes a nuisance of himself? He throws his clothes around, refuses to help out around the house and pesters his little brother perpetually.**
>
> I would seek to find a way to link his behavior to something important to him, such as privileges or even money. If he receives an allowance, for example, this money could provide an excellent tool with which you can generate a little motivation.
>
> Suppose he is given $4 a week. That maximum can be taxed regularly for violation of predetermined rules. For example, each article of clothing left on the floor might cost him a dime. A deliberate provocation of his brother would subtract a quarter from his total. Each Saturday, he would receive the money remaining from the taxation of the last week. This system conforms to the principle behind all adolescent discipline: Give the individual a reason for obeying other than the simple fact that he was told to do so.

I know it seems severe to you to think: No car because of some dumb chores or stupid piano, but read the article at the left from Dr. Dobson. His magazine arrived today and in my mind— a God-send. It certainly drives home all the things I have been trying to explain to you. Well, all I can do is continue to guide you in God's truth.

    Love,
    Mom

Friday, Oct. 25, 1996

Dear Candi,

Last night I was so tired, I couldn't make an entry. I guess I was perturbed about my account missing over $400. Well, today I realize where it is and I feel better. My Father had been watching over me all that time.

Today, at the hairdresser's, I was very pleased that as worldly as our hairdressers, Trish and Sonia, are, they realized the wisdom of your obeying me. You tried so hard to show them how hard, mean and unfair I am, but I have to believe that deep down, you know I am right. They have not been our hairdressers as long as you have been my daughter, yet they seem to be able to acknowledge good parenting when they see it.

Tomorrow is the last day of cross country and it's not so much that I don't want you to enjoy a party with your friends, but have you taken a look at your room? That dresser is so filthy. Of course, we can't even mention the carpet. But then again, you didn't ask for a white carpet in your room.

However, you did ask for a piano and you did ask for Benji. They are still not being taken care of. Well, I do know that I sound like a broken record. This is the reason why I am using this journal as a sounding board.

Love,
Mom

Having started the journal, I wrote in it almost every day. I only missed one which I explained by stating that I was very tired. I am sure that my weariness was from the constant struggle and battle with Candi and being unable to account for the missing funds in my account. I discovered that the missing money was due to a bill that I had paid twice. The person later returned the check.

You might be curious about the conversation with Trish and Sonia who had been our hairdressers from many years. Candi started complaining to them about how I wouldn't let her do anything; how I was very irritating in nagging her about her chores and wouldn't leave her alone. Trish and Sonia both right away told her that she was blessed to have such a good mom and that she should always be respectful to me and do what I asked of her.

Up to this point, the biggest issue I had with Candi was her chores not being done. However, her falling grades soon became a greater issue and she, in turn, made other things become problematic. She would whine and complain about playing a song during the offertory when Pastor asked her to do so. I really don't think she complained because she didn't like the people or because it was burdensome. I think it was all part and parcel of her anger against the Lord and her rebellion against what I desired for her.

Candi wanted her own way about everything. As she approached her sixteenth birthday, she became fixated on getting her license and a car right after that. She felt a right of entitlement for all the amenities that most teenagers desire. She wasn't able to see that hard work, good behavior, respect, and adhering to some established protocol were prerequisite to achieving her desired goals.

As you read through the entries, which are pretty much self-explanatory, you will see that Candi's issues were not solely confined to those things that I have enumerated here. You can pretty much see that it was a no-win situation. Still, as a parent, I did not give up. I continued to seek answers in God's Word, and through books and other articles which gave a measure of Godly counsel. Prayer was my chief weapon. I don't think I have ever prayed more in my life than I did during those difficult years with Candi.

Saturday, Oct. 26, 1996

Dear Candi,

    I am sorry that you had to miss the final party at Coach S's house. I still can't believe that all these little privileges are being taken away from you and you are still not heeding the warning. You even seem not to be taking the advice of Trish and Sonia. The Bible says: Wise men see danger a far off and flee from it ... (from Proverbs 27:10 NCV).

    Look at your room. It is still so filthy and you didn't clean it. I had to remind you to pick up your clothes off the bathroom floor.

    You haven't even looked at Benji. If I don't take him out for exercise, he doesn't get any.

    I know you are struggling with your courses, but you are not dedicating enough time for studying. Apparently you are not too serious about anything.

    Well, here I go again, nag, nag, nag. I guess I just can't help it. I am glad we move our clocks back tonight as I really need the extra hour of sleep and so do you.

                                     Love,
                                      Mom

Chapter Two

UNBEARABLE TENSION

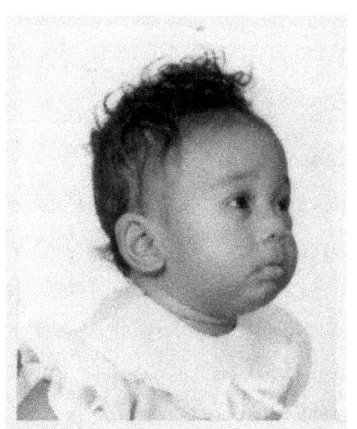

Candi age 3 months

Sunday, October 27, 1996

Dear Candi,

I am really surprised at you. One would have thought that with all that you have happening in your life: changes at school, difficulty with courses, our relationship, your relationship with God and so on, you would want to do something about it, but apparently not.

Right now about 5:40 P.M. I am in the bathroom looking at your dirty clothes on the floor; your room is filthy, Benji's poopy corner is filthy and he hardly has any water in his bottle. You fed him today only because I reminded you to.

You are doing nothing that I can even feel like you are trying. Well, he who has ears to hear, let him hear, says God our Father. I wish you were hearing, but I guess you prefer to pay the price.

Love,
Mom

P.S. I just have to add this footnote. You were so rude and disrespectful today, yelling and without any regard for me and my authority. I wanted to slap you so hard, because the Lord says:

> Honor your father and your mother, so that you may live long in the land the Lord your God is giving you.
> Exodus 20:12

How quickly you forget. But, I restrained myself because I am reminded of the other scripture:

> [Parents] provoke not your children to wrath..
> Ephesians 6:4 (KJV)

I will tell you this, though. These past few months you certainly have been honoring your dad. I'm glad. You know, it wouldn't be such a bad idea for you to go and live with your father, whether here or wherever. May God forgive me, but if that should happen, amen, so let it be. You would never live with me again. You would have made a choice that I would make sure you keep until you are an adult.

Monday, October 28, 1996

Attitude
By Charles Swindoll

"The longer I live, the more I realize
the impact of attitude on life.
Attitude, to me, is more important than facts.
It is more important than the past, than education,
than money, than circumstances,
than failures, than success,
than what other people think or say or do.
It is more important
than appearance, giftedness or skill.
It will make or break a company...a church...a home.
The remarkable thing is we have a choice every day
regarding the attitude we will embrace for that day.
We cannot change our past...
we cannot change the fact
that people will act in a certain way.
We cannot change the inevitable.
The only thing we can do
is play on the one string we have,
and that is our attitude...
I am convinced that
life is 10% what happens to me
and 90% how I react to it.
And so it is with you...
we are in charge of our attitudes."

That includes me, you & your Dad!

Tuesday, Oct. 29, 1996

Dear Candi,

I have been worried about you. I am not worried because I think God is not in control, but I am worried about your response and reaction to everything.

I can't explain why it is now, at this particular phase and during this period of our lives when things have come to a head, but I don't get angry; instead I am learning to lean more heavily on my Father.

Please, Can (Candi's nickname), remember God has said, He will never leave us nor forsake us (Deuteronomy 31:8, and Hebrews 13:5). He has also said, you will never see the righteous forsaken or his seed begging bread (Psalms 37:25).

Candi, what wonderful promises! I only wish for you to continue to pray and trust God as I am learning to trust Him.

I hope that on Saturday when you go to the University you will understand the math and physics a little better. Thank God for providing you a University tutor.

Love,
Mom

Wednesday, Oct. 30, 1996

Dear Candi,

It was so nice to see you happy and pleasant today. I just praise God for the mighty work He is doing in your life.

I am so glad you called Dennis (piano teacher) for a little help with your piano lessons. I pray that you will lean more heavily on your Father and know that He is the Lord and God of your life.

Love,
Mom

Thursday, Oct. 31, 1996.

Dear Candi,

Well, Honey, two days and you have been so sweet. You're back to your old self.

Thank you for putting out the sign for the trick or treaters.

I'm glad you had an opportunity to talk with your coach. Well, I've got to go. I'm so tired.

Love ya,
Mom

P.S. I think God made it so cold tonight to deter the trick or treaters.

Friday, November 1, 1996

Dear Candi,

Before I started tonight (9:04 P.M.), I asked the Lord for a promise for you and this is what He gave to me:

> His compassions fail not.
> They are new every morning.
> Great is thy faithfulness.
>
> Lamentation 3: 22 & 23

The explanation on the other side said:

> "Great is thy faithfulness"
> O God my Father
> There is no shadow of turning with thee.

Candi, God has been so faithful to us. Have you thanked Him that He is providing for us in an abundant way? Your dad is gone with his hefty paycheck, but you can't say that you are lacking for anything. Give Him praises, Honey. I don't feel like telling you anything about chores tonight. I just want to encourage you to earnestly seek God. Live for Him and trust in Him.

I am so grateful to Pastor for going over and paying for your Regents Exam. Although he is the pastor, remember he is a fallible human being and he did this favor with the joy that comes only from the Lord.

Let's give God a mighty praise on this cold night.

Love in Him,
Mom

Sunday, November 3, 1996

Dear Candi,

I didn't write in your journal yesterday because we left early to go to the University and then to Grandma's, your aunt's and the mall. Of course you had to put Chris' keys in my purse and we had to go back to Grandma's to drop them off. After grocery shopping, I was too pooped to drop you a line.

Now, it's 9:41 P.M. which is still pretty late, but at least we got your videotape done for AP Physics class tomorrow.

(Candi, along with three other classmates, were grouped together to complete a visual around the Doppler effect and to identify and calculate sound waves at varying speeds. They were able to create an interesting visual, videotape it, and finish the project amidst the many other assignments and extra-curricular activities)

The song we were both listening to in the car is still reverberating in my head:

> Only by grace can we enter
> Only by grace can we stand
> It's not by our human endeavors
> But by the blood of the Lamb

Gerrit Gustafson © 1990 Integrity's Hosanna! Music CCLI 190579

I can't remember the rest of it, but I hope and pray that you will always remember that it is only by God's shed blood that we have any eternal hope. The best thing that ever happened in my life is the day that God called me and I responded. It hasn't always been a joy ride, but it is always a comfort knowing He is always right beside me. The trials and tribulations have been hard and difficult at times, but God promised that your grief will turn to joy. I do hope that you will get to the point where the joy of the Lord will be your strength.

Love,
Mom

Tuesday, November 5, 1996

Dear Candi,

Today I am writing with such heaviness of heart. I truly feel as bad as I would if my best friend had died and gone to hell and the pain of knowing that she was totally and eternally separated from God was beyond anguish.

I don't know if you recall your telling me last week that you went to bed and dreamed that the Rapture came. You woke up in a cold sweat and rushed to my bedroom to see if I were still there. You said you were so relieved that I was sound asleep because you rationalized that the Rapture could not have occurred since I was still here. I wonder if that could be a warning? I guess you should ponder a little bit more.

I had to reread my entry on October 28th on Attitude where Chuck Swindoll says, "We can't change the past." Candi, I wish I could; not so much for my sake, but for yours.

Last night was a big argument over your grades, your

attitude and getting help. You resist everything and I see you lashing out at me to blame me for everything. Yes, I take the blame, but life goes on and I will still continue to honor God, rely on His strength, and be the mother to you that He wants me to be.

There are many things I could have told you and never did, but I will tell you one now. Candi, your dad is hurting too, I know, but his hurt comes from a bad decision he made years ago.

When I got pregnant with you years ago in Jamaica, your dad refused to marry me and I lost my job. You see, teachers could not be pregnant out of wedlock. I could have fought it through the Union, but I was too embarrassed to do so. Thank God, my mother filed my papers and I came here.

Immediately when your dad saw a chance to come to this country, he agreed to marry me to get his papers. Yes, I agreed to marry him too. Stupid, ah!! Well, what can I say? I rationalized on the basis that you would have two parents and things would seem normal to the rest of the world. How wrong I was!

The bad part in all of this is that your dad missed out on the person he truly loved, the person he wanted to marry. I know he regretted the decision that he made and hates me as well as himself for the horrific façade and masquerade of a marriage we fought to maintain.

The Jehovah Witness thing, I believe, is your dad's attempt to find peace. I wish he could open his eyes and realize that this peace can only come from God.

You are probably wondering why I am telling you all this. Truthfully, I don't know, except to say that it is my little way of trying to make you understand that there is no hope of reconciliation with your dad. You think that by us getting back together, things would be fine, but I have lived long enough to know that it would be a horrible situation for all three of us.

Today, after your outburst, I realize that you are in for some serious problems. I truly expect for you to fail a lot of courses, and frankly, I don't expect at this time and at this moment that you are going to get into a good college. I foresee a very difficult road ahead for you, but it is the choice that you have made. I think maybe I have tried too hard on my own to shield and protect you, so now I am leaving it in God's hands.

With God's help and if I am still alive, I will be able to provide you with a little food and shelter. The rest will be up to you.

I know I brought you into a bad situation, but I have provided a solid, Godly foundation. I am sure you realize that your dad does care for you and I do, too. You probably don't believe the latter, but at least I haven't abused you and I gave you the best that I could.

Hopefully, some day you will realize the truth of Psalm 27:10-11 "Though my mother and father forsake me, the Lord will receive me. Teach me your way, O Lord; lead me in a straight path ...."

That was the Psalm that comforted you the night your dad told you not to call him Dad anymore. Candi, there are many people in a worse position than you are. Rebelling is not the answer. God says: Call upon me in time of trouble....

Instead of wasting your energy blaming me and pouring out your anger on me, look to God. Only He alone can renew your strength and give you hope.

I have never felt more like going home to be with my Father than now. At least if I weren't here, you could live with your dad and you wouldn't ever have to be upset that we weren't a family. At least you would be comfortable knowing that I was dead, which would make that desire for us to be a family again, null and void. I don't worry though, because God knows best and will make things transpire as He orders them. May God open your eyes some day soon!!

In Christ,
Mom

P.S. It is amazing how you make time to go watch the soccer game and go everywhere else, but according to you, you have done all you can to get good grades.

Candi's Grades

As people read this little memoir, they are probably wondering why it seemed as if I were putting so much pressure on Candi to get good grades. I will explain. After the divorce, Candi brought home her progress reports and I noticed that for math she was getting grades like 110% or 115%. To me, this was unheard of for a junior. When I asked Candi the reason for such ridiculous grades, she said that they were bonus marks or extra credits. I made an appointment to speak with her counselor. I was informed that my child scored a perfect score on the math Regent's exam in tenth grade.

My next question was, "So why isn't she in the honors program?" After some he-hawing, I demanded that she be placed in the program. I was informed that Candi would need to work extra hard to catch up because there were some things that the advanced group had already studied which Candi's group, the accelerated program, had not yet been taught. Well, in a calm and respectful way, I made sure everyone was aware that I was not pleased. Lest, you, the reader, didn't get this, Candi was present at the conference.

Well, they moved Candi to the honors group and that is when more problems started. I never saw her putting out any effort to make up for lost time, and she began bringing home grades like 60%, 65%, etc. When I attempted to speak with her, it always ended up in a shouting match. She would tell me that she was a dummy and I had no right to change her from her math group.

At the same time, she started having some difficulty with biology. I had gone to the school and told them that Candi was not allowed to participate in any part of the curriculum that dealt with evolution. The teacher had informed me that there were probably only about two questions on the exam that dealt with evolution, so Candi's grade would not be impacted much. Yet somehow they were being affected.

Candi was participating in the S.T.E.P. (Science & Technology Entry Program) at the University, and thank the Lord, she loved it. I spoke with someone in the program and asked for tutoring for her. A time was set up for Saturday mornings at 9:00 A.M. Of course, that clashed terribly with cross country, indoor track, and many of her extra-curricular activities. There was a hissy fit, but, thankfully, it was short lived.

Now I was putting up with Candi's low grades in addition to her chores not being completed, her not practicing her piano, her rabbit not being taken care of, Candi being upset at not getting her way with Driver's Ed, and upset at there not seeming to be any plans afoot for getting her a car. If she were miserable to live with before, she became twice as incorrigible.

Thursday, November 7, 1996

Dear Candi,

    I feel an urge to stop writing to you, but I will continue so that should anything ever happen to me, you would have a little reminder to help push you in God's light.

    I won't remind you about chores and other things because I know you already know that you are not doing them. You know there is a verse in the Gospels where Jesus told Peter that Satan desired to sift him like wheat, but He had prayed for him.

    Can, Satan is sifting you and I am praying for God to strengthen us and give me wisdom to deal with your rebellion, disrespect and resentment. I hope that in the end, you will truly look back and realize how much God truly loves you.

    Have fun in Connecticut with your dad.

Love,
Mom

I was coming to the end of my rope. After that argument and her outburst that I mentioned on November 5, Candi was so rude, angry and disrespectful that I once again contacted Dr. James Dobson and asked for help with counseling for her. A counselor from Focus on the Family called to talk with me and suggested that I meet with a Christian psychiatrist and counselor at the University. I contacted the doctor, left a message and he later returned my call. We had a long conversation on the phone before he actually met with Candi. I felt that he wanted to evaluate what kind of a Christian I was, in order to tailor his talk with Candi around the principles in the home with which she was being raised.

I contacted my health insurance and they approved a total of twenty-six visits for Candi. The hope of what the appointments would accomplish helped carry me through the next few weeks.

Chapter Three

WILL THE COUNSELING HELP?

Candi age 3

Friday, November 8, 1996

Dear Candi,
    I came home today and you had already left with your dad for Connecticut. I hope you both have fun together.

                        Mom

Sunday, November 10, 1996

Dear Candi,
    I didn't realize that you weren't coming back from Connecticut until tomorrow. I am glad you had this weekend with your dad. I also hope that you had an opportunity to minister to him and make your light to shine.
        Well, I guess I will see you tomorrow, God willing.

                        Mom

> Tuesday, November 12, 1996
>
> Dear Candi,
> You just told me that I said you had until November 27th, your birthday, to get your math grade up to a "B." Fine, I am willing to be flexible. Please sign below and on the 27th I will call Mrs. Clarke and if your grade is not a "B," you are OUT of indoor track.
>
> Sign: _Candi Bogues_
>
> _Lorna Bogues_
>
> 11/12/96

You see, I made the call: good grade first and everything else after. Later, Candi started getting straight A's which continued for the rest of her junior and all of her senior year. Her counselor even sent me the paperwork that would allow her to complete college math courses while still attending high school. Candi wasn't interested. She said she wanted to enjoy high school and not feel pressured with school work all the time. I didn't force her to do it. I chose my battles. Now, here is the million dollar question: Was Candi a dummy?

Thursday, November 14, 1996, 9:00 P.M.

Dear Candi,

    I am writing in pink ink because it is cold and I am very comfortable in bed and I don't want to go downstairs.

    Well, I am glad we had that talk last night, after band. It was truly wonderful to see your dad participating in your concert, after being totally separated from almost everything in your life for over four years.

    Well, I had to go get my Daily Bread out of your room, so I also got the pen.

    I hope that with prayer and supplication before God, you will see that Satan wants to sift us, and we cannot allow him to get into our midst. Of course, the only way to avoid that is to put everything before our Father.

    Well, our two hour talk last night has taken its toll. It seems that on one hand you know what you are supposed to do, but there is this force that propels you in the wrong direction. If you would only look to the Lord, you would be less aggrieved and more apt to see the truth. I am dying to sleep, so I am taking an early night. I hope there won't be too much snow on the ground tomorrow, so driving won't be so bad.

                                              Love,
                                              Mom

Sneaker Incident

One of the things that I became very cognizant of was the need to truly be Christ in Candi's eyes. You see, she was watching for any opportunity to point out that I also faltered in my walk with Christ. It isn't that I had to be perfect, but Candi wanted her own way. She was looking for a chance to accuse me of using a double standard, that it was okay for me to respond in a negative way, but when she did likewise, it was a problem. In other words, she was waiting to find any flaw in me to use as a weapon against me.

When a little incident occurred at the Sporting Goods store, I felt the need to clarify. I wanted her to understand that when I erred, I owned up to it, asked for forgiveness, changed the behavior, and moved forward.

Candi bought a pair of Nike sneakers for track, but by the second time she wore them, they fell apart. There was a definite flaw in the product. I called the company and they wanted us to mail the sneakers to them, which we did. They sent us back a comparable pair of sneakers. Candi hated the color, and the style was slightly different.

I called the company again. They said we could take the sneakers to any of their stores and exchange them for something more appealing. We chose to go to the store closest to us. They didn't have a pair of sneakers like the particular style we were sent, so the salesperson said we could choose another pair and pay the difference in price. The manager agreed and scanned the box of the mailed sneakers. Well, lo and behold, that box rang up for less than half of what we had originally paid for the defective sneakers! The manager wouldn't listen to us. He was not even willing to negotiate. I was livid. I took the sneakers, went home and just seethed.

I was very upset. I felt that these huge companies assemble these sneakers in China for pennies, sell them to the general public for a fortune, and when they are at fault; they are not willing to solve the issue amicably.

I should have just taken the matter to the Lord, waited until the next day, called the headquarters for Nike like I had done before, and see if a solution could be achieved; but I didn't. Instead, I called up the manager of the store, gave him a piece of my mind, and hung up before he could reply. Then I felt rotten to the core.

I felt like the Ruach HaKodesh (Holy Spirit) was saying to me, "Great job, Lorna. What a perfect example for Candi. When you are upset, don't try to work things out amicably through dialogue. No, just blow your top. Show your ignorance. This really solves the problem and leaves you feeling like the woman that you are, right?"

It is hard to explain how this little incident ate at my insides. I truly felt terrible. I felt that I owed some explanation to Candi, and I did apologize to her. Still, I felt that I needed to make a recording in her journal, so that later she could read it and put things into perspective as the Lord directed her.

Friday, November 22, 1996

Dear Candi,

I know you think that I am just a miserable mother, but can you imagine? You were home today while I was in school for Superintendent Conference Day, and none of your chores were done.

Wasn't that manager at Dick's Sporting Goods really testy! He made me so mad, but I am wondering if in my impatience, I misrepresented God.

God says:

> A soft answer turneth away wrath:
> But grievous words stir up anger.
>
> Proverbs 15:1 (KJV)

Maybe we should have just taken the sneakers away quietly and said thank you. Anyway, I will get you the pair of sneakers that you really want. No one can rob God and all that we have is His. I don't feel like going through the hassle of mailing back these sneakers and waiting for a solution which may or may not be to our liking.

Love,
Mom

I LOVED YOU ENOUGH...
For Our Teenagers —

Some day when my children are old enough to understand the logic that motivates a parent, I will tell them:

I loved you enough to ask where you were going, with whom, and what time you would be home.

I loved you enough to insist that you save your money and buy a bike for yourself even though we could afford to buy one for you.

I loved you enough to be silent and let you discover that your new best friend was a creep.

I loved you enough to make you take a Milky Way back to the drugstore (with a bite out of it) and tell the clerk, "I stole this yesterday and want to pay for it."

I loved you enough to stand over you for two hours while you cleaned your room, a job that would have taken me 15 minutes.

I loved you enough to let you see anger, disappointment and tears in my eyes. Children must learn that their parents aren't perfect.

I loved you enough to let you assume the responsibility for your actions even when the penalties were so harsh they almost broke my heart.

But most of all, **I loved you enough** to say **NO** when I knew you would hate me for it. Those were the most difficult battles of all. I'm glad I won them, because in the end you won, too.

(Author Unknown)

Counseling Appointment

The day of the appointment with the Christian counselor finally came. I drove to the hospital, and Candi and I started walking to our destination, the doctor's office. Well, the big sign said, Psychiatric Center. As soon as we saw the sign, a few individuals whose behaviors were less than we would consider normal walked past us. My little Angel blurted out, addressing no one in particular.

"Whoa, Candi, Loony, welcome to the Looney Bin."

I immediately tried to reassure her that this was just an opportunity to speak with a Godly individual who would be able to provide some perspectives on her issues. My words fell on deaf ears. She didn't acknowledge that I had even spoken. She just stared straight ahead and totally ignored me.

We found the office, registered, and sat down to wait our turn. Fortunately, we were the only two people sitting in this tiny waiting area. Candi was as stiff as a board. She acted as if I weren't there and refused any of my overtures to engage her in conversation. We sat there like two strangers in absolute silence. It seemed like an eternity before the doctor came out, but it was probably no more than ten minutes. The doctor greeted us and introduced himself. He said he would be with Candi for about an hour. Candi did extend her hand to the doctor's outstretched one, and she followed meekly behind him as they went toward his office.

Incidentally, Candi was never disrespectful to any other person, except for my very dear friend, Dawna, and me. I think she targeted Dawna because Dawna was such a dear support and dedicated friend to me, even though the latter never saw the full depth of Candi's disrespect and rebellion. Candi's teachers thought she was just the most wonderful, young lady. Her report cards always said, "A pleasure to have in class." I guess I should be grateful that at least I didn't have to worry about teachers calling to complain about her.

Well, what do you know? Candi was actually smiling when she came back to the lobby. I was shocked and flabbergasted, but happy. Maybe things were going to be different, after all. No, things did not change, in the short term. But today I am pleased to see the Godly young woman that God has crafted from the old mold.

The counselor said he wouldn't share with me the content of the discussion he had with Candi. He would leave that up to her to do so. But he did tell me that Candi was secure in my love for her and that she directed all of the anger and frustrations she had for her father, toward me because she knew that no matter what, I would always be there for her. His words gave me hope which I held on to and still respect to this day.

He said that he really didn't feel the need to see her again, but he would schedule one more visit, which he did. That second visit lasted less than an hour and although Candi's behavior toward me did not improve, I am now able to understand, many years later, the wisdom of his diagnosis. I admire his integrity in keeping Candi's therapy brief. I marvel that secular counselors will have their clients coming back repeatedly, day after day, for years, with minimal, if any, results.

To this day, the only information that Candi has shared with me is that as she was walking behind the counselor toward his office, he suddenly whirled around and said, "So, Candi, you think you are the only one who has been angry with God? So were Job, and Moses, and Elijah and David and...." She couldn't recall all the characters that he named.

I am eternally grateful to Dr. Dobson for his Godly wisdom and for the counselor at the University whose Godliness and faithfulness to the Word of our Heavenly Father have helped to mold and guide my daughter. Today she is a very sweet, lovely and caring young lady who understands the need to look to the Lord for guidance, help and direction. Need I explain how this came about? It was God. Let me tell you. God is faithful and even though the storm clouds in your life may seem frightening and overwhelming, trust Him. He is patient and longsuffering, and He never leaves us.

I just have to pause and in hindsight reflect on something that I have heard and have often pondered. God is never early, but He is never late. He arrives just in time. Romans 8:28 is a verse we should all memorize and recall, to help us keep focused. *"All things work together for good for them that love the Lord and are the called according to His purpose."* Today as I look back and reflect on all the difficulties of Candi's emotional turmoil, I wouldn't want to repeat it, but I wouldn't change who she is today for anything. In the end, it all worked out for good.

Coach S

In addition to the counseling and a great youth group at church, another positive thing for Candi was that she loved sports and actively participated. It was a blessing because in Coach S, she found a father figure. She did cross country and track, both indoor and outdoor, so she had a lot of time to interact with Coach S. She opened up to him and he loved her. He wasn't a Christian, but a decent human being who took a lot of interest in all of his students. He had parties and many social events at his home which gave him an opportunity to keep his students focused and occupied. Today, I see so many children whose only socialization is the television or questionable, unsupervised hanging out with friends. My grandmother's favorite expression is so true: The devil finds work for idle hands and minds.

With Candi already angry, I felt there was no reason to provide any further opportunities through the lack of a structured schedule for her to be influenced by those peers who would lead her toward a decadent lifestyle. Coach S planned supervised activities that allowed his students to socialize, share, and discuss issues related to school, sports, family, etc. Under his guidance and tutelage, his students learned to grow and flourish.

Like anything in life, when you love and respect a person, you are more apt to desire to please that individual in whatever you do. Candi pushed herself to achieve and to improve to get Coach S's approval. She had tried so hard to please her dad, and I am sure she felt that she had failed. Now, she could actually work hard and have a father substitute acknowledge and affirm her achievements. I am truly grateful to this fine coach. Yes, I know this world is changing and people have to be vigilant and cognizant of the motives of acquaintances, even if that person is a teacher. How blessed Candi and I were to have a coach whose interest was solely for the social and emotional well-being of his students!

Sunday, November 24, 1996

Dear Candi,

    Incredibly, in a few days you are going to be sixteen years old. I know you do feel a great sense of accomplishment and excitement. I try so hard to understand your elation because I remember how I felt many eons ago.

    I am glad that we had that talk last night about your dad. I hope you do see God's hand and His great love for us.

    I wish that you could understand that my sole purpose and desire is to see God's will and, through His strength, do it.

    At least you agreed that we should both start praying for your dad.

                                    Love,
                                      Mom

Tuesday, November 26, 1996

Brrr!! It is freezing cold.

Dear Candi,

    You know, tonight I am feeling a real sense of nostalgia and sadness. It's so hard to believe that you are practically all grown up. Goodness, it seems that only yesterday I was bringing home a tiny wrapped bundle of God's goodness and blessing for me.

Well, Can, you are on your way to becoming a young woman. Pretty soon you will be on your own, i.e. going to college.

I know the last few months have been quite difficult for us, but God hasn't forgotten us, and His light has been shining exceptionally bright for us to see, but unfortunately, sometimes we have not yielded as we should.

I know you probably can't understand why it seems that I haven't grieved over our situation as you have, but remember that grieving is a stage. I think there are five and if I remember them correctly, they are:

- denial & isolation
- anger
- bargaining
- depression
- acceptance

Of course, you must remember that I have had a longer time to deal with this, so I am at the stage of acceptance.

I hope as you turn SWEET SIXTEEN, you will make sure the sweetness pours out and you will look to God as Master, Savior and Lord of your life. I can't wait for you to get to the point where you will feel comfortable to make a public commitment (baptism) to Christ. I believe that you would truly see the power of God more clearly.

Well, Honey, this is truly the start of a very different phase of your life. May God always be a part of it.

Love in Him
Mom

Wednesday, November, 27, 1996

Happy Birthday Can!!!

    It is quite a cold, snowy day. In fact, the roads were quite bad driving in to work that I wondered if I would make it back home to get you and take you to the hairdresser.

    Did you see God's hands, though? Your filling fell out and so your dad had to get you and take you to the dentist. Then after cleaning up my classroom, I was able to get you and take you to Sonia's by 2:30. I didn't have to drive home because you were already in the city.

    Well, it wasn't much of a party, but Ivette, Anthony and Raphae made it worth the while.

    I am glad you like your sixteen pink carnations. I love you and I know you realize that your Heavenly Father loves you so much, beyond our simple understanding.

    The last few months have been rather difficult times between us, but I hope that with God's help and His continued presence, leadership, and direction in our lives, we will understand that through His love, He will lead us always in the path of righteousness.

    On the next page I am pasting an article by James Dobson that has helped me.

54 Defiant Daughter *Divine Grace*

Dr. Dobson Answers Your Questions

Q. You have said that your philosophy of discipline (and of family advice in general) is drawn from the Scriptures. On what references do you base your views, especially your understanding of the will and the spirit?

A. The dual responsibility assigned to parents appears repeatedly in the Scriptures but is addressed most clearly in two passages:

• **Shaping the Will:** "He [the father] must manage his own family well and see that his children obey him with proper respect" (1 Timothy 3:4, NIV).

• **Preserving the Spirit:** "Children, obey your parents in the Lord, for this is right. 'Honor your father and mother'—which is the first commandment with a promise—'that it may go well with you and that you may enjoy long life on the earth.' *Fathers, do not exasperate your children; instead, bring them up in the training and instruction of the Lord*" (Ephesians 6:1-4, NIV, emphasis added).

Significantly, this second Scripture instructs children to obey their parents but is followed immediately by admonitions to fathers regarding the limits of discipline. We see an identical pattern in Colossians 3:20-21: "Children, obey your parents in everything, for this pleases the Lord. Fathers, do not embitter your children, or they will become discouraged" (NIV).

A parent's relationship with their children should be modeled after God's relationship with man. In its ultimate beauty, that interaction is characterized by abundant love—a love unparalleled in tenderness and mercy. This same love leads the benevolent father to guide, correct, and even bring some pain to the child when it is necessary for his eventual good.

Hebrews 12:5-8, 11 tells us: "'My son, do not make light of the Lord's discipline, and do not lose heart when he rebukes you, because the Lord disciplines those he loves, and he punishes everyone he accepts as a son.' Endure hardship as discipline; God is treating you as sons. For what son is not disciplined by his father? If you are not disciplined (and everyone undergoes discipline), then you are illegitimate children and not true sons . . . No discipline seems pleasant at the time, but painful. Later on, however, it produces a harvest of righteousness and peace for those who have been trained by it" (NIV).

Why is parental authority so vigorously supported throughout the Bible? Because the leadership of parents plays a significant role in the development of a child! By learning to yield to the loving authority (and leadership) of his parents, a child learns to submit to other forms of authority that will confront him later in life.

The way he sees his parents' leadership sets the tone for eventual relationships with his teachers, school principals, police, neighbors, and employers. These forms of authority are necessary to healthy human relationships. Without respect for leadership, there is anarchy, chaos, and confusion for everyone concerned.

These questions and answers are excerpted from the book Dr. Dobson Answers Your Questions, published by Tyndale House Publishers, Inc. Dr. Dobson is president of Focus on the Family, a nonprofit organization dedicated to the preservation of the home. His daily radio program is heard on more than 1,400 radio facilities in the U.S. and Canada. If you would like a copy of the radio broadcast listing or the monthly Focus on the Family magazine (both are distributed free of charge), write: Focus on the Family, Colorado Springs, CO 80995.

I know that you hate discipline, but read again this article from the Biblical perspective and see if you can understand things a little better.

Friday, December 20, 1996

Dear Candi,

    I don't know exactly what the temperature is outside, but it is bitingly cold and the below zero wind chill can almost be felt in my nice, comfortable bed.

    Today on my way home on the bus with the kids from their skating fieldtrip, I was reading my Sunday school book and something jumped out at me. They were talking about resentment and bearing a grudge and how left to fester, they destroy the individual.

    Well, the article was a bit long, so I copied it and decided to cut out the most important and significant parts. Read carefully and apply.

by Keith Drury

Have you been hurt deeply? Ever? By whom? Has this personal injustice ignited resentment in your heart? Has your resentment turned into a grudge?

When someone hurts us, we are inclined to settle the score, get even. If we do not forgive the offender the choice remaining is to try revenge, or decide to hold a grudge. Revenge is an outward attempt to even the score. A grudge is revenge turned inward. But a grudge doesn't work.

In getting even with another, we hurt ourselves – spiritually and emotionally, perhaps even physically.

Holding a grudge will eat at your insides. Eventually you will become a bitter person. All this happens because you refuse to forgive the one who hurt you. The price is too high. It's not worth it.

A grudge handcuffs you to the past. Holding a grudge keeps life running on rewind. You keep looking over your shoulder at some past injustice you experienced. You recall how awful it was. A grudge handcuffs you to this negative past, causing you to blame your present failures on past misfortunes.

Resentment left to itself flickers and dies out. It must be fed to be kept alive. Where does this fuel come from? It comes from your own mental and emotional energies.

A grudge usurps God's rightful role. The ultimate sin in an unforgiving spirit is that we take God's authority from Him. God, and God alone, has the right to condemn men and women. Only God has the right to hold another accountable for sin. Vengeance is His exclusive domain. When we refuse to forgive another we raise ourselves to the level of God, as if we can hold another under charges for their sin. Forgiveness allows us to turn this account over to the ultimate Collector of debts.

God calls us to forgive one another as God forgave us (Col. 3:13).

Hate the sin, but love the sinner enough to forgive him or her!

> Have you been hurt? Has someone been unjust to you? A parent? It is in the willing to forgive that you can actually forgive. You can do it. You can! In one single transaction you can determine that you will no longer consider that your offender has an "outstanding balance" with you. The debt is "history" . . . cancelled . . . **paid in full** – turned over to the Eternal Debt Collector. Not because they were right, but simply because you want to obey Christ

Spiritual Discipline for Ordinary People, Keith Drury, Wesley Press, 1989

Candi, I couldn't very well highlight everything; although all is important. A few are just so strikingly, overwhelming and exactingly true that I just gave the added emphasis.

I didn't want to lecture you, so I didn't name any specific situation, but if there is any truth to this, the Holy Spirit will bring conviction.

Love,
Mom

9:07 P.M.

Chapter Four
MY LITTLE GIRL IS BACK!

Candi age 3 1/2

Youth group trip: The Wesleyan Church that both Candi and I attended usually had their youth exposé, the day after Christmas. In 1996, they went to Philadelphia.

The time that Candi was away gave me time to ponder getting her a car. She had turned sixteen and now she could focus on nothing else except Driver's Ed and the prospect of getting her own car for her senior year. I knew that she really wanted a car and with the Lord's help, I wanted her to have one, but not if she would continue her disrespect. I wrote out my plan, but keep in mind that I didn't voice any of this to Candi at the time.

Saturday, December 28, 1996, 9:12 P.M.

Dear Candi,

I hope you are having a grand old time in Philadelphia and more than ever I hope that the Lord is speaking to your heart while you are there.

Today was surprisingly quite warm. In fact, I think the high was 51°F, so I was quite thrilled when Jean called to see if I wanted to go for a walk. It was quite a pleasant walk and while I was walking I was thinking about your car and what would happen when the time came to purchase it. God laid a scripture on my heart and I just opened my Bible and read it. This is what it says:

> Bring the whole tithe into the storehouse...
> and see if I will not throw open the floodgates of heaven and pour out so much blessing that you will not have room enough for it.... And you will again see the distinction between the righteous and the wicked, between those who serve God and those who do not.
>
> Malachi 3:10-18

You will probably need to read all the verses from 10-18 to fully grasp it, but the bottom line is, Candi, that when we are obedient to God and follow His statutes and commandments, He keeps us in peace, harmony and prosperity. When we are disobedient, then you know all that can happen.

Therefore, since you are unwilling to do what Christ would do, I will purchase the car in my name, as soon as you find a job. Each month, you will give me the car payment. You see, I have to be a good steward and if I didn't do what was right in God's sight, like the servant with the one talent, God would take it away from me.

As soon as you start truly living for Christ, God will bless your effort and He will open the floodgates of Heaven and reward you handsomely.

Love,
Mom

My Sweet Candi Was Back

Candi was so excited when she got back from the youth trip to Philadelphia. She had gotten to see Ray Boltz whose song, "Watch the Lamb," she really loved a lot. She bought the tape for me, as well as a t-shirt with a picture of what people perceive Jesus to look like, with his arms stretched out wide and a crown of thorns on His head. The caption said: He loved me this much that He stretched out His arms.

Candi was so bubbly and full of life and excitement when she got back. She couldn't stop telling me about all the fun things that she had done and the exceptionally good time that she'd had. She was so much like the old Candi and I was thrilled listening to her recount everything.

She kept going on and on about how much fun Julie was—one of the chaperones. Julie was young and full of life. She was one of our church's youth leaders whom Candi admired and loved with a passion. I know first hand that she really was a blessing to her young protégés.

Candi's time with the youths from many different churches and the renewing of her relationship with Christ was truly a blessing. It was a time for all those young people to reflect on their walk with Christ. They had great youth leaders to encourage and wow them into sticking close to the Lord who is our constant companion and has always promised to be by our side. Candi needed that. She also needed the time of reprieve from me and the issues that plagued her/us. And it was wonderful to see her come back with sparkling eyes and childlike excitement.

Her excitement was contagious. Even though I hadn't attended, she shared so much that I actually felt like I had participated in their fun. She loved the theme which was, "What would Jesus do?" It was so befitting our situation that I was just as thrilled as she was. It was so good to see her bubbling with joy—Godly joy. And it was so refreshing to have this little glorious time of reflection together.

Having her come back from Philadelphia somewhat changed, really motivated me into praying and seeking God for a car for her. But for some reason, I didn't share these thoughts with her.

Wednesday, January 1, 1997

Happy New Year   10:45 P.M.

Dear Candi,

    I'm glad you had a great time in Philly as well as at the New Year's Eve party with the two Wesleyan youth groups.

    There isn't anything earth shattering that I want to tell you, except that I have made one resolution for 1997. I plan with God's help to not make any decision until I find out, "What would Jesus do?"

    I have to tell you that I know that this is going to impact every decision that I make for you and for me. I wish that you would make a decision like that, too. I really believe that you would really see God's hand in a really new and exciting way. I wish you would stop and reflect on how wonderful God has been to us in the past year. I just can't imagine the great things He has in store for us during this coming year.

    Please, Can, continue to love and trust God. He has said He will be a father to the fatherless and you know how He has proven several times that He will take care of us.

In Him,
Mom

Forbidden Movie

Candi and I had another opportunity to bond—a few quiet moments together to grow closer to each other and to the Lord. It only happened because of unforeseen circumstances orchestrated by our Heavenly Father.

This touching mother/daughter moment occurred because of a sleepover that Candi had at her friend Ann's home one Friday night. Candi had asked if she could see the movie, "Scream." Now, need I tell you that I vehemently objected and forbade her to see it. Of course, while she was at Ann's, she went to see it anyway.

The Lord has ways of reprimanding us that we cannot imagine. The following night, I went to bed and so did Candi. Well, about 3:o'clock in the morning, I felt these arms encircling my waist and heard this hiccupping kind of sobbing. It was Candi.

"Mom, I can't sleep. I keep seeing the fear on the young people's face as they were hacked to death."

I listened further as she recounted many of the horrors she had seen. We talked about why it is not good to watch those kinds of movies. Then, there in the darkness, we prayed. Later we snuggled down together and went back to sleep. It was so much like the old Candi, the child I knew and loved. It was a glimpse of better days gone by. I didn't scold her for disobeying me. I think she had already figured out the wrong she'd done.

I always tried not to chide Candi by saying, I told you so. I still feel that whenever someone says, "See, I told you," it is really a gloat that undermines any relationship. Whomever the statement is directed toward, already knows that you had told him or her so. Even though it was true that I told Candi things several times and she still didn't listen, I have never said thus to her. However, I am sure she herself has reflected many times, Mom did say such and such.

Sunday, January 5, 1997, 9:00 P.M.

Dear Candi,

Today I can see that God is working in our lives and especially in yours. After watching the movie, "Scream" (and you know Jesus didn't go with you), I guess you could clearly see God's hands—we actually had another rare opportunity to pray together. Boy, it's such a treat to experience such novelty.

Well, today is quite a telegraphic note because I want to go to sleep. I wonder if you are planning to come crawling into my bed again tonight (*~*). Well, you can come, but do be quiet.

Love,
Mom

Chapter Five
ORANGE PEELS AND BASKETBALL BOY

Candi, kindergarten

7:47 p.m.
Sun Jan 12, 1997

Dear Mom,

I am sorry for the way I have been acting lately. That also includes my rudeness and selfishness. I have been unfair in expecting you to be everywhere I want you to be. It's just that I see my other friends and both their parents at every meet or soccer game no matter the weather conditions or how busy they are. I see this and think that you should be at every event I participate in. I know that you are a single parent and that you are working twice as hard to support me with everything I want. I know you can't be everywhere at once, but it is just that this year I have improved so much from my freshman year of indoor. I have other team coaches asking coach Sc____ what my name is because they don't remember our school having too many girls win their races. My chances of making Meet of Champions is much greater. Getting on to my point though, you seem to always point out my weaknesses. You don't seem to notice my improvements such as doing my chores, practicing my piano, and going to bible study. Sometimes you take things I do the wrong way. For example, just a few minutes ago I went to touch you on the shoulder and you backed away saying you were very angry with me now and that I was very close to being slapped. I was only trying to get you to look at me.

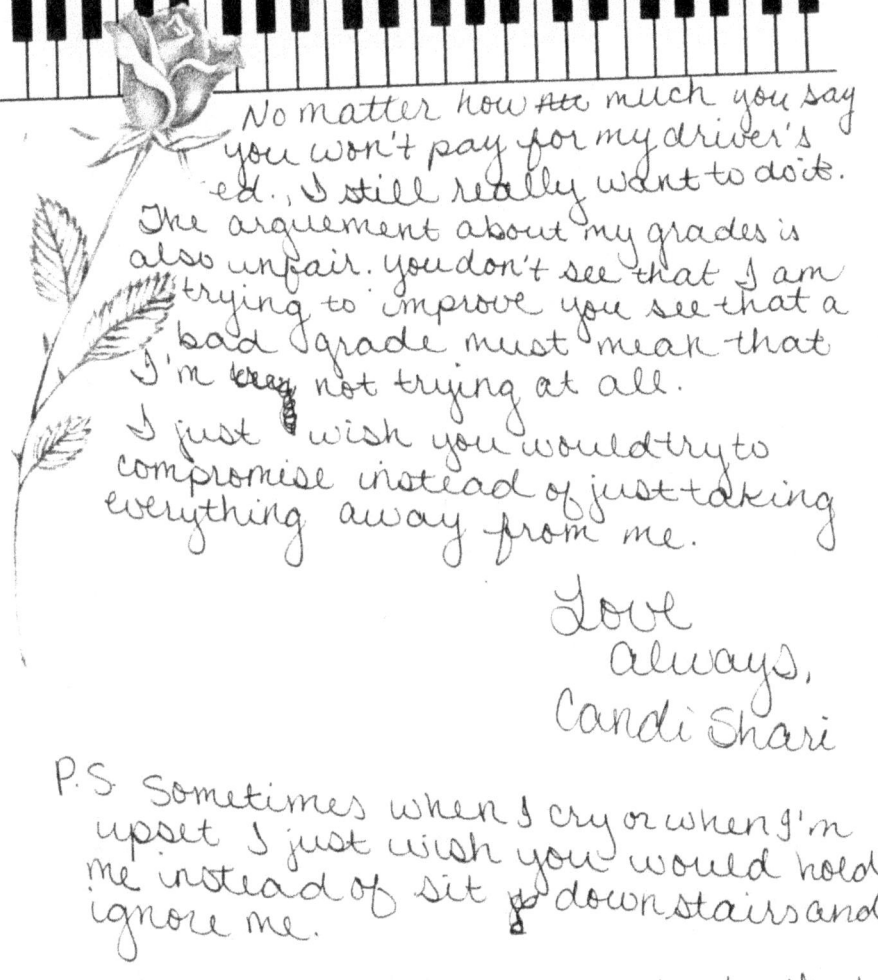

No matter how ~~mu~~ much you say you won't pay for my driver's ~~ed~~., I still really want to do it. The arguement about my grades is also unfair. You don't see that I am trying to improve you see that a bad grade must mean that I'm ~~try~~ not trying at all.

I just wish you would try to compromise instead of just taking everything away from me.

    Love
     Always,
      Candi Shari

P.S. Sometimes when I cry or when I'm upset I just wish you would hold me instead of sit ~~g~~ downstairs and ignore me.

"How good and pleasant it is when brothers live together in unity!" Psalm 133:1

"For if you forgive men when they sin against you, your Heavenly Father will also forgive you. But if you do not forgive men their sins, your Father will not forgive your sins." Matthew 6:14,15

      Candi

This letter from Candi truly showed more about her than the actual words she wrote on the page. Knowing that I knew the reason for Candi's behavior, based on the psychologist's diagnosis back in November, one would think I should have been more understanding. I tried, honestly I did, but it is difficult to put into words how unreasonable Candi was.

If you are a parent, you can most likely relate to this. Candi did cross country, indoor and outdoor track, plus the ten thousand other activities that juniors and seniors get involved in. She expected me to be at every track meet and social event that was planned. But that was not always possible. I was a teacher. I had other responsibilities and obligations. But if I missed one thing on her schedule, I had to put up with hissy fits and tantrums. I had long since learned that reasoning with Candi wouldn't get me anywhere.

Candi wanted to complete her Driver's Education and she wanted me to see that she deserved to have a car. She felt like she was truly trying to do well in the academics, in sports and in her chores. Hidden in the midst of her ranting and raving in the letter, one can identify the pain of other issues that she was dealing with. One of which, of course, was acceptance and affirmation. She wanted me to affirm her good efforts and I feel that I did try hard to do that, but it just seemed that good times with Candi never lasted. I was always on pins and needles wondering when the next outburst would strike.

I wanted so much to listen to her and hold her and hug her, especially when she was crying. I cried and cried when I read that part of her letter. Even now, as I am writing this, tears are welling up in my eyes. I longed to go back to the times when we could snuggle close while we read our Bible and prayed together. But I couldn't wade through the morass of Candi's disrespect and get past the rebellion to the hurting child, in order to hold and comfort her as often as she would have liked or as often as I wanted to.

It is hard to explain how much stress and tension I was under. You see, I had no human support to lay all my burdens on. I am sure I could have shared with some of my Christian friends, but I knew that people get tired of that sort of thing very easily. It's human nature. They don't want to listen to complaints and negatives all the time. The Lord's shoulder was the only one I leaned on during those dark times. He was the only one that I felt safe burdening.

Sunday, January 12, 1997, 9:51 P.M.

Dear Candi,

    I have just read your letter which I will include in this journal, so sometime in the future you can come back to it and reflect on what you wrote.

    I am not trying to be mean and unfair like you say I am. In fact, it's just the opposite. You probably believe that I just make any old haphazard decision when it comes to you. But you should know by this time that, as far as possible, I put them before our Father.

    Your dad's and my relationship came to a head when it meant choosing between him and God. Of course, you know the end of that story.

    Please remember that with God's help whenever it comes to choosing between Him and someone else, I will always choose according to His word. If I weren't doing that then I never would have sought help from Dr. Dobson and the counselor. God does say to seek Godly counsel.

    I know you can't understand when I say that I am tired, but I am. This past Saturday, I could have come to your meet. It was just that I had already planned to go to Canada and I had gotten up early to listen to the weather report. I know you get upset when you see families together and ours is ripped apart, but God is in control of ours. I will be at your meet next week and I will reserve more time to be with you.

    I love you, Can, with all my heart, but my first responsibility is to God. I must do what He decrees first.

                                     Love always,
                                     Mom

Saturday, January 18, 1997

Dear Candi,

    I hope you have fun sleeping at Ann's tonight. I am so glad we were able to work out a fair compromise. However, after that big blowout last Saturday and Sunday, things look a little bit uncertain. So, I decided to draw up our contract. So, here goes.

> Honor your father and your mother
> that your days may be long upon the
> land that the Lord has given to you.
>
> Parents provoke not your children to wrath.

So said; the foundation of the contract is:

I, Candi, promise to put God first in everything. I will respect my parents especially my mother (mostly because I live with her and therefore have more interaction with her) and will speak things/matters/problems out in a positive way or write them down.

Should I revert to the behaviors I displayed this weekend: rudeness, disrespect, shouting and giving God second best, then I will not do Driver's Ed until this summer and will get a car during the summer of 1998. This also means that I will behave like a young lady and carry out my duties as expected.

Sign: __Candi Bogues__

        __Lorna Bogues__
                      Mother

A Car

Well, now you see what I mean about being on pins and needles wondering when the next outburst would strike. It struck! This one was most likely about the car. She was relentless. It was a recurring theme that she played back over and over again. You can see from her letter on January 12 that she was not about to let up. Her quest for a car and Driver's Education started long before age sixteen was in sight. However, things intensified when sixteen was actually a reality. Prior to her dad becoming a Jehovah's Witness, I had promised Candi a car when she got her license, but, of course, the situation had changed drastically since then. I was now a single mother. Maybe she fought it so hard because she thought that getting a car had become an elusive, financially impossible dream.

I bet most people didn't know that a right of passage for most seniors was that they could no longer ride the school bus once their school year started. That was Candi's contention. How did I expect her to ride the school bus? Her friends were going to be driving and she was going to be the only one without a car. The ONLY one, Candi? Oh, how she hated my sarcasm!

The Weekend Blowout

I don't remember the particular "blowout" I mentioned in this journal entry. I didn't always write down every single awful moment. Frankly they would have been too numerous and frequent to record. Instead, I just touched on some of the significant ones in which I wanted to really scold her and teach her. I would have loved to talk to her face to face, but knowing that it would only turn into a screaming match, I just wrote.

Orange Peels

The next journal entry reveals another such outburst. I had always prepared a lunch for Candi. She would put the school's menu on the refrigerator and write, "buy" or "bring," so I would know when to make her a lunch. Well, on this particular day, I made her lunch and the fruit was an orange. I would always peel the orange and remove the pith for her. For whatever reason that I can't recall, I did not remove the pith that day. Oh, Candi was livid. She came home and ranted and raved. How did I expect her to eat her orange with the white stuff still on it! Even now as I am writing, I cannot adequately express or address clearly her disrespect and the tone of her voice.

I am pretty sure, that you, the reader, might think I am making this all up. I wish I were. Suffice it to say, the Spirit of the Lord was with me. I didn't yell, and I didn't slap her. In the quietest voice I could muster, I simply said, "From this day on, you will make your own lunch."

> Wednesday, January 29, 1997
>
> Dear Candi,
> Tonight was quite a little scene and you truthfully almost lost the opportunity to do driving lessons. Well, at least from now on you will be peeling your own oranges since you expect me to do it completely according to your standard, at all times.
> Sometimes I think you forget that you are sixteen. Anyway, a simple little grounding is in order for this weekend and you will just have to make your own sandwich on Friday.
> It is such a shame that ever so often you revert to your little attitude. Well, try not to lose out on all your little benefits.
>
> Love,
> Mom

I don't remember much about what followed. I know that I didn't make her lunch for a while. Candi tells me now that I did go back to making her lunches again. So I am assuming she must have apologized or begged me to continue and I did. I am pretty sure it wasn't right away, though.

I want this little journal to be a work of reflection, so now I am reflecting. I am sure now that it wasn't the pith that Candi was angry about. I am guessing that her outburst over the orange was triggered by something else. Maybe it was a smoke screen which masked the real problems she was having in school—problems that I didn't learn about until later.

I can't change anything now, but sometimes I wonder how I should have dealt with those times. However, in all my pondering, I still don't have a complete answer.

Candi was not the type of child to open up and speak. She kept a lot of her feelings bottled up inside and would just explode at the slightest provocation. Even just reminding her to feed her rabbit or mentioning any other mundane thing could initiate a negative reaction.

Sometimes, as I look back, I think it was probably just as well that I didn't react to her outbursts. I think she needed time to work through the issues for herself. I know that if I had tried to reason with her, it would have only been an open door for her screaming and blaming which would have done nothing to soothe her or calm my anger.

Today Candi reminds me that I did often give her the silent treatment. It wasn't deliberate on my part, but it seemed like the only way to have a semblance of peace in my home. I cringe now at how this must have affected her. She was hurting so much and then to have me ignore her must truly have been a lot for her to bear. For that I am truly sorry. I never said I was a perfect mother. Thank the Lord for His forgiveness and for Candi's today.

As I said, I spoke very little directly to Candi when problems occurred. However, I have informed her, now that she is grown, that I did speak. I spoke through the journal which I handed to her when she left for college. Although my responses were not always immediate, she did learn and has finally come to understand how things were affecting me. She also came to the realization that I did understand her hurt and her pain.

Trouble at School

Approximately a week after the incident with the lunch scene, I found out that Candi was having some problems at school with a girl by the name of Melissa. This girl belonged to the popular "in" crowd. For reasons unknown, she started picking on Candi. Apparently, as Candi was running for track practice, Melissa was sitting with her group of buddies on the sidelines, and as Candi jogged by, she stretched out her foot and kicked her. When I learned about this incident, I was incensed. Candi, however, did not want me to go to school and do anything about it. She was right. It's not good for kids to have their parents fight all their battles for them. I learned from Candi that this was a one-time event. Thank God for that.

Thursday, February 6, 1997   9:01 P.M.

Dear Candi,

I think you misunderstood what I was telling you tonight. This girl Melissa (I think that's her name) had no right to hit, punch, or kick you. Sometimes I think you are just too soft. As a teacher I have observed that the so-called big, bad bullies pick on a person they perceive they can manage and manipulate. I am so angry inside that I almost feel like I should go and retaliate on your behalf.

Of course, I know I have to leave it to the Lord. I wish you had decided to go to the Christian School. I know you would miss your friends, but at least you wouldn't have to be preoccupied with mean, selfish and uncouth beings like Melissa and her cohorts. I am surprised that Shannon is a friend of hers. I guess kids do change a lot between elementary and high school.

I hate to say this, but I bet she never would have picked on one of those tough, inner city girls. Then again, we know that she is a coward.

I love you, Honey.

Love,
Mom

Basketball Boy

It is necessary to also note here that the incident with Melissa came shortly after another school-related incident. A certain basketball player took a liking to Candi. I didn't get any indication from her that she had any feelings toward this young man. We had talked about him before. She had told me that he was a rather promiscuous person and she had no interest in him. Thank God, Candi was not into sex, drugs, or alcohol. However, two cousins liked this basketball player and imagined Candi to be a threat to them.

The two young ladies, who were a part of the Urban Suburban program, decided to bully Candi. Now, this is how misguided society can be. Candi had no relationship with this basketball player except as a peer, yet these two girls, instead of focusing on why they were being spurned by this student, decided to bully the person they perceived to be the object of his attention.

They started threatening Candi. They even pulled her hair one time! Another time they followed her into the girls' bathroom with the intention to beat her up. Candi was aware of their intention and stayed in the stall for a long time, missing her class, because she was afraid to come out. Thank the Lord for His mercy, they left without hurting her.

It had only been a few months earlier that, at a nearby inner city middle school, a female student was stabbed by another female student over a boy! She died. And these girls threatening Candi were from the inner city! Candi must have been terrified every day as she approached school, knowing she would have to face those girls.

Just as an aside, if you do not understand the Urban Suburban program, this is what it's all about. Students who attend the inner city schools can apply for acceptance in certain suburban school districts. Upon acceptance, they are bused to that particular district for their instruction.

When I heard about what was happening to Candi, I was furious. I certainly did not want Candi to ever be placed in a dangerous situation! I knew that Candi, though she could be defiant towards me, did not know how to defend herself against this kind of thing. She was not a fighter—not vicious at all. It worried me how much of a pushover she was when it came to her peers.

I sent a letter to the school officials about it, but nothing changed. Therefore, I felt it necessary to meet with school personnel to ensure that proper precautions were taken to safe-guard my child whenever she was on school premises. I spoke vehemently to the vice principal that I paid taxes in this town so that my child could be in a stress-free environment to study without having to worry about her life being threatened! I said that something had better be done about it before she gets hurt! Soon after that, these students were called to the office and were reprimanded. They never bothered Candi again. Of course, a few weeks later, those same two students had a big fight in the hallway and, based on their record, were suspended from the program. Was God being a Father or what?

Well, with those and other issues impacting Candi's life, I wanted her to change schools and attend a Christian High School, but she wouldn't hear of it and I understood her reasoning. Here she was, almost a senior. She had gone to school with the same set of students since first grade. To start in an environment where she would be the new kid on the block was certainly not appealing to her. I am sure it would not have appealed to most other people either.

Those were not the only two incidents. A later school-related problem, dated June 4th, 1997, needs no further explanation or clarification. You can judge for yourself.

Now, let's go back to Candi's favorite subject, the car. Remember, she still hadn't gotten her license as yet, but she was certainly paving the way for this car that she was bound and determined to have. Also remember that she was unaware that I had been trying to figure out how to get one for her. From her point of view, it looked like I was determined to refuse her wish. The next journal entry demonstrates the lengths to which she would go, to ensure that she would get a car when the time came.

Orange Peels And Basketball Boy

Here I am in my element as a teacher.
This was taken during that stressful time.
You can sort of read the strain on my face.

Chapter Six
ALMOST TO THE BREAKING POINT

Candi age 7 and Lorna

One day Candi's dad called to confront me about not providing enough food for Candi. According to him, based on the conversation with his daughter, she wasn't getting enough to eat and furthermore, I was hiding things from her. This of course, was her way of trying to ensure that the funds her dad provided for her would be diverted to procuring a car for her.

Tuesday, February 18, 1997

Dear Candi,

Tonight seems to be a defining moment in our relationship. If anyone would have told me a year ago that this could have ever been a possibility with you and your dad, I would have emphatically denied the suggestion.

How could you lie to your dad about things being hidden from you?! What have I been hiding from you? You claim you couldn't find the pop that your dad bought in Connecticut, but did you ask? They are still sitting in the garage.

After this incident of Candi complaining to her dad about not having enough to eat, it seemed that our relationship took a nose dive. She was mouthy, more disrespectful than before, and if it were possible twice as rude as she had been.

It was almost like the dry period between the book of Malachi and Matthew. I didn't make another entry until April 29th and as I reread now what I wrote, I am a little embarrassed and quite sad that such negativity was recorded in the journal, but maybe it just shows that I'm human. I hope so. It seemed like the arguments and disagreements with Candi were now occurring on a daily basis. In attempt to keep the peace, I spent a lot of time praying and just plain ignoring Candi—even more than I had before.

One day she called for me to come and get her along with some of her friends and drive them all home. Now, Candi's friends were great kids. She'd had that close inner circle of friends since the first grade, so it was never an issue for me to do things for them. Their parents were equally wonderful to Candi. Usually when I picked them up I would be most cheerful and cordial, but on particular this day I was a little reserved. Later Candi told me that her friends were so surprised. They wanted to know what was wrong with me and where my sunny personality had gone. Thank God that today they still communicate with me. I think they have come to realize what a handful Candi was.

License at Last

Well, one of Candi's big days arrived. She got her driver's license on April 16. In her mind there were rights and privileges that came with such an achievement, but Mom wasn't cooperating. Her incessant nagging was now accompanied with rancor and ire, peppered with sassiness as she became mouthier than ever. It came to a head when she crossed the line. I don't remember what she said. All I can remember is storming into her room, grabbing the telephone from her and slamming it against the wall. My journal entry and her letter of apology will give you a sense of both our feelings at that time.

Hopefully, you can see, as you read between the lines, that her letter wasn't a true apology. It was just a way to continue to promote her agenda, the car. Dropped rather carelessly in between the lines is, "I am sorry for my rudeness," immediately followed by, "…but the car." That was quite typical of the true nature of my wonderful child at that particular phase of her growing up years.

Dear Mom,
   You've told all the time that we should pray and do what the Lord wants. When you wanted the hairdryer, you prayed about it, but you also went looking for one. With the car, you can pray about it, but haven't even attempted to look for one. What about the verse seek and ye shall find. If you are not looking then how are we supposed to find a good bargain for a decent car? Not many things you have received have fallen out of the sky. Another thing that hurt me was the night you said I only had a crush on John. Well you

seem to think that Rob and I are going to get married. (which I can tell you from right now, isn't going to happen). I know there is no chance I will marry John, but doesn't mean I can't <u>like</u> him. (notice how I said like and crush). Yes I know my attitude has been very disrespectful lately. I also know that you could ~~move~~ make me move in with Dad (that doesn't mean I want to). I am sorry for my rudeness, but how you can't even compromise with the car? Let's say ~~if~~, and I do mean if, we went to check out a car we brought a mechanic with us? It is just a suggestion. We could also ask people at church if they know anybody who is selling a car. Hopefully their friends would be more honest than a total stranger. Well I did start this letter out to apologize for my rude behavior. Oh guess what? Last night when I went to bed, I opened my bible up to James (I think) 3:20 and it children obey your parents. Well I have class now!

Love,
Candi

P.S. the verse was Colossians 3:20

Tuesday, April 29, 1997

Dear Candi,

I haven't written a note to you in a while and it's not because things are good, but because they have been so bad, I haven't had the energy, fortitude or desire to put anything on paper.

You got your license on Wednesday, April 16th and you have allowed satan (I have to write it in lower case) to twist and sift you.

Last night I honestly wanted to wring your neck, but God gave me self-control. I couldn't believe that you apologized on Saturday; Sunday you were somewhat rude and on Monday you were an obnoxious, facetious, disrespectful little jerk. Well, I guess it's your fault that it was the phone that connected with your wall and dented it. Frankly, I believe that if it were not for the Spirit of God really dwelling in me, it would have been your body doing the connection and getting the bruises.

Let's see how long this written apology will last. I plan to glue the letter in here.

I wish you could take your eyes off the world for a moment and seek God's direction for a car.

I am not asking you to marry Rob. I know he likes you and he is a good and dedicated Christian young man. I wonder which parent wouldn't like to see his/her child being interested in someone who would encourage him/her to continue to grow and be strengthened in the Lord.

Love,
Mom

The Phone Incident

Telling moments like this one, depict to me that when we are going through changes and we feel set upon on every side, we often do not respond with intellect or wisdom. I felt battered and torn and unfortunately I did respond emotionally at times. This particular time I certainly blew it. I wish I would have used self-control. I think I was often patient and understanding with Candi, but like Moses striking the rock instead of speaking to it and instead of striking the people, I slammed the phone instead of Candi. Was I correct in my response? Of course not, and I am not justifying my behavior either. Like I have said once before and I will reiterate, I am only human. I hope, though, that everyone can see how the Lord was faithful. It is only the Lord's grace that kept Candi and me from losing our sanity.

Candi's Point of View

Here's Candi's e-mail response in 2009 to this question from a friend of mine: "How did you feel about your mother's reactions to your negative, rebellious attitude?"

> "That's easy to answer. If my mother was annoyed at me, it was quite obvious to everyone outside looking in. You could cut the air with a knife, literally. Until I apologized for my rude behavior, my conversation with my mom involved very few words. For example:
> Me: Hi, Mom.
> Mom: Good morning, Candi.
> Silence for about 5-10 minutes.
> Me: Bye Mom.
> Mom: Bye Candi.
> Many notes were written between the two of us because it was easier to get everything out without having to deal with awkward silence. I must have said "I'm sorry" so many times that I sounded like a broken record to my mother."

(See more reflections from Candi on page 132.)

My Students

One question that friends often ask is how I was able to be productive in my job, when I was under such emotional strain with Candi. Of course, my answer again is the Lord. I love teaching and the Lord gave me students that, for the most part, really loved me. I poured out all the love and affection on them that it seemed like I wasn't able to pour out on Candi. I gave to them and they received in a way that Candi was not able to appreciate, stuck in the level that she was at the time. I looked forward to going to school every day. Seventh and eighth graders can sometimes be a lot of fun. I had students who would ask if they could come to my classroom during lunch time and sit with me. We played games together.

I had one very mean, sassy kid who threatened to punch me. In his anger, he balled up his fist and came at me from all the way across the room. I stood my ground without flinching, although inside my heart was pounding. When I reported him to the principal, he denied it, but since all the other students backed me up, he was disciplined. One day during gym class his shirt got ripped all the way down the seam in the middle of the back. He came to my classroom and refused to leave because he was embarrassed. I went to the home and careers teacher, got some needle and thread, and sewed up his shirt. Need I tell you that he became my best friend after that?!

I had my students write in their journal for ten to fifteen minutes each day. I would take their journals home, read them, and I always wrote a response. The kids loved it. They would pour out their hearts to me. I became their counselor and advocate—like a second mother. If I ever did not get to the journals to make a response, they would become so upset. In fact, I tried to cut back on the amount of time I gave them to write in their journals, but it didn't work. They needed that interaction. I formed a bond with my students.

I always listened to Christian radio during my planning time and lunch time, and my students became so curious about Jesus. I could share with them what the Lord had done in my life and they were so receptive. I often wonder what students would be like if we didn't have separation of church and state. Most likely, we'd have a society where law and order would be practiced and respected.

I could relate story after story of how God gave me favor with my students. Our Savior has promised that He will never allow us to be tested beyond what we are able to endure. It would have been too much to have a miserable job and be miserable at home, all at the same time. Therefore, He gave me joy and fulfillment in the work that He had called me to do. I got up every day with renewed excitement about going to work. It was coming home that caused some level of anxiety. As I got closer to home, I would usually get that tight feeling in the pit of my stomach. I had to face Candi and, most likely, it was not going to be a pleasant experience.

Chapter Seven

JEALOUSY TRIANGLE AND A BLUE CAR

Candi in high school

Candi has always been a very social butterfly and had a host of friends, both male and female. I have already said it, but it bears repeating here. Candi was not into sex, drugs, or alcohol. Her quest was not to destroy herself. She was just determined to drive me crazy, torture me, or at least make my life miserable.

Well, she became close friends with another student, Brian. She started sharing little things with me about his girlfriend, Katie, with whom he was having problems. I guess she gave him her opinion which I am assuming he shared with his girlfriend. Well, Candi soon started having problems with Katie, who had transferred from a private high school in order to be with Brian. I counseled Candi to distance herself from Brian. But, of course she didn't listen, in spite of the many conversations that I had with her.

Wednesday, June 4, 1997

Dear Candi Bogues,

I guess it is a joy not having to write to you every day, but to just sit back and watch you prove me right (*-*).

I am sorry about today, but I told you to stop associating socially with Brian and now Katie is actually threatening you. As a Christian, you can actually say hi and walk on; do not make small talk with him.

I am glad you are going to be much older when you read this, so you won't have to pout because I told you so.

Now, you understand why I desire a Christian college for you. The world is changing. People are solving their problems through violence and I don't want you to be the recipient.

Well, let's see if you will go to school tomorrow and ignore infantile, moronic, imbecilic and immature Brian and his insecure and lovesick girlfriend.

As I am reflecting and writing this now, I am amazed at the rationale that some individuals have. If a wife or husband (or boyfriend or girlfriend in this case) is being indiscreet, why confront the other individual? Focus on the perpetrator and resolve the issue with him or her. I knew that Candi and Brian were just friends, but Katie didn't. She felt threatened. Someone had told her that Candi was secretly in love with Brian. She, in turn, accused Candi of trying to break up her and Brian's relationship. Trying to protect her claim on Brian, she set out to hurt Candi by spreading rumors that would turn Candi's friends against her. Katie's poisonous lies did not impact Candi's true, inner circle of friends with whom she had parties, get togethers, and sleepovers. However, another acquaintance with whom she used to play soccer did side with Katie which really hurt Candi. She came home quite upset. In the end, Candi took my advice and distanced herself from Brian by not sitting with him in the cafeteria, etc. Of course, after all that, by the end of the school year, Katie and Brian broke up.

Fending Off Car Battles

Well, with God's help and mercy, the school year ended with Candi getting very good grades and even managing to end up on the honor roll. The community always printed all the relevant school information in a newsletter and mailed them out to all the parents in the district. It was really a pleasure to see Candi's name included as an honored scholar.

Although Candi and I did not communicate much because of the constant battle regarding chores and everything else that she wasn't doing, she took the initiative and went out and got herself a job. She now had extra money to do a lot of things, and she was allowed to use my car, as long as she bought the gas. Since I do not work during the summer, she was always driving some place. I tried not to make an issue of that, but it was hard. I knew that with God's help, I had to get her a car of her own; otherwise, using my car would soon become another major battle.

In August, she went to Hawaii with her dad for vacation. While she was away, I found a car, a little blue Honda Civic hatchback. It was waiting in the garage for her when she got back.

Monday, August 25, 1997

Dear Candi,

    I am sure you are going to be thrilled when you get back from Hawaii and find that you have gotten a car. God is a faithful Father and even when we don't have time for Him or are not committed enough to make a public stand for Him, He still stands for us and never disowns us. What an awesome Father! Today, or when you read this, you can reflect on what a Great and Loving Father you have.

    I can't tell you how hard I prayed and what a difficult decision it was to get this car, but our Father understands and He found This Car for you. Please make sure the music and the conversation in His property always bring honor and glory to Him. Read the parable in Matthew 25: 14-30. If we are not good stewards of what God entrusts us with, He will take it away and give it to those more deserving of it. On the following page is a little secular article that I found. It does have some wisdom to it. Please read faithfully, trusting in our Savior.

                                  All my love,
                                  Mom

DEMOCRAT AND CHRONICLE ■ SATURDAY, MAY 3, 1997

Nursery-rhyme advice keeps young drivers safe

ANN LANDERS

Dear Ann Landers: I found this little verse in my husband's old driver's ed book from 1973 (author unknown). My stepson is nearing driving age, and we keep it stuck on our refrigerator. Although the advice is almost 25 years old, it is still sound, and I hope you will run it in your column for all drivers out there — young and old.
— Stepmom in Winston-Salem, N.C.

Dear Stepmom: That takeoff on an old nursery rhyme may be a lot more effective than a lot of preaching. Thanks for sending it on. Here it is:

Ten Little Drivers, cruising down the line. One had a heavy foot, and then there were nine. (Speed limits are set for your safety.)

Nine Little Drivers, the hour was getting late. One dozed a moment, and then there were eight. (A tired driver is a dangerous one.)

Eight Little Drivers and the evening seemed like heaven. One showed his driving skill, and then there were seven. (Drive sensibly and sanely at all times. A car is no place for a clown.)

Seven Little Drivers, their lives were full of kicks. One bought a bottle, and then there were six. (Gasoline and alcohol are a deadly mix. Don't drink and drive.)

Six Little Drivers, impatient to arrive. One jumped a traffic light, and then there were five. (Don't gamble years of your life to save a few extra seconds.)

Five Little Drivers, wheeling near the shore. One viewed the scenery, and then there were four. (Careful driving demands alertness at all times. Keep your eyes on the road.)

Four Little Drivers, happy as could be. One passed a car on a hill, and then there were three. (Never pass another car when your vision is obscured.)

Three Little Drivers, busy it is true. One neglected car repairs, and then there were two. (For safety's sake, keep your car in top condition.)

Two Little Drivers, and the day was nearly done. One didn't beam his lights, and then there was one. (Slow down for dusk or darkness. Adjust your driving to existing conditions.)

One Little Driver, who's still alive today. By following the safety rules, he hopes to stay that way.

The Car

Oh Candi was as pleased as punch with the car! She was able to go to school and submit her name for the lottery. There were some designated parking spaces on campus exclusively for students. You needed to show documentation, submit your name, and hope you were one of the two hundred and fifty lucky students who would get to park on school grounds.

Yes, Candi did get her parking space. She also finished the Driver's Ed course so she could drive after 9 p.m. She was on cloud nine.

In giving her the article by Ann Landers, I couldn't be accused of nagging. After all, it came from a renowned individual who sure knew a lot more than Mom.

Grandma

In September of 1997 my mother, Candi's grandmother, was in a serious car accident that left doubt as to whether or not she would ever walk again. Everyone took turns helping her out a little. I would leave work and then go to assist in whatever way that I could. Often, I wouldn't get home until late and frankly, during those times, my relationship with Candi was mostly positive. I believe that having someone else on which to focus was good for us both.

Candi's Dad

As I reread the following journal entry, it gives a little glimpse of what my relationship was like with Candi before the divorce. Sometimes I try to imagine what life would have been like for her had her parents not divorced. I guess I will never know. I might not have had as mouthy and rebellious of a child. But on the other hand, having experienced our situation, I know she could still have been a somewhat angry person who would have dabbled and indulged in activities for which I know she would have had regret as an adult. One reason I say this is because of what her father was like.

When Candi's dad became a Jehovah's Witness while he was still living with us, he was attempting to put a tremendous amount of pressure on Candi: no hanging out with friends, absolutely no interaction with the opposite sex, spend time reading the Bible or the *Watchtower*, and spend more time within the "family" (other members of Kingdom Hall). With all that, Candi still one day accepted a ride from a male friend. When her father realized that the school bus had gone by without Candi on it and saw her waiting for this ride, he took her in his car part of the way to school, reprimanded her, and made her walk the rest of the way. This was in the middle of a cold, winter day!

This was rather typical of how he treated her. Therefore, I imagine that had our home remained divided, it might have caused Candi to be angry and to make some questionable, irrational decisions which could have negatively impacted her life in the long term.

Later, Candi's dad decided that her going to the local community college while working to pay for her own courses would do just fine for her. I thought otherwise. I knew Candi had a good aptitude for learning and does well when challenged. She needed an environment where she would have a full semester load of activities, structured routine, and deadlines to get things done. The Lord knew what was best for Candi. In the divorce settlement, the Lord worked it out that Candi attended a good college and both her parents had to pay for it.

I know that during the college years, away from the scrutiny of parents, many young adults make some serious mistakes that often come back to haunt them years later. Thankfully, Candi was spared that, in spite of, or maybe because of the divorce.

Thursday, November 27, 1997

Dear Can,

Happy birthday! I am sorry that I am not home for us to have breakfast together, but I know you understand that I have to help your grandmother.

The little excerpt below came from a story that Dr. Dobson related in this month's newsletter (or magazine). I felt that it was quite succinct in expressing what my God-given responsibility as a parent is for you.

You can plan what you want us to do this evening. We have already watched "Drop Dead Fred." Oops, pardon me. I watched it; you slept.

Anyway, we could have a late night. Put one of the sparkling grape juice (Martinelli's) in the refrigerator and we will sip "champagne" (did I spell it correctly?), and watch a movie, even if it is "I Love Lucy."

I love you, Honey, and may you always remember that it's God's love, grace, mercy and strength why we have been able to endure this far and why you have been granted another year.

Love you always,
Mom

Happy Birthday!

> You can introduce Christ to your kids, even lead them to the Lord, but only they can reach out and take His hand. Your duty parents, is to present Christ to your children. He will do the rest. Then, on that Day you'll hear Jesus say the best words a parent can ever hear: "Well done, my good and faithful servant. •

two hearts that beat as one

Chapter Eight

MUSIC AND EARRINGS

Candi age 4

I am amazed, looking back now, how few journal entries I made during Candi's senior year. I know that it isn't because things were so incredibly wonderful. The next journal entry certainly proves that. Our battles had not changed much. We were still struggling with the same issues, but with her new-found independence having a car, we weren't in each person's space as much as before. Thank God. She was pretty busy and often wasn't home, so we had less time to get into conflicts which was probably for the best, and which is most likely why I didn't write as much.

However, I couldn't keep still when her defiance took a little different twist. She knew what the rules were for the house, but she still tested them and tried to get her own way. You would think she would have known what my reaction was going to be before trying anything, but that was my daughter, Candi. She always had to test the limits with her mother.

January 2, 1998, 10:48 A.M.

Dear Can,

It's a new year and for many people new beginnings. I am sorry it seems that we have started out this year on such a bad footing. However, this short note is really to reiterate and reinforce things that you already know.

Candi, I don't know what it is you want, but it is obviously not what I want. I don't want you to be like me. In fact, I would have only liked for you to worship and serve the Lord, but like your dad, you have to make your own choice.

Please understand that you cannot do as you please in my house. You are approaching eighteen and like the story of the Prodigal Son, in the Bible, you may leave this house any time you wish. I will be talking with your dad on Saturday. After our talk, if he continues to give me a check, I will sign it over to you and if you wish to find an apartment or live as you please outside of this house, it will be up to you.

Understand that I am not trying to throw you out. You can live here until you are eighty as long as you are willing to obey my rules. But, all of a sudden you are playing a bunch of secular music. Feel free to choose your lifestyle. Worship whomever you please, but as with your dad, not in my house. If I am wrong, God will deal with me. I will serve Him 'til the day I die, but I will not force anyone else to do so. I will say again though, I will not share my blessing with anyone living outside of Christ.

Can, just let me know what it is you plan to do. I just want you to know that I am not angry. I only feel angry and upset when you try to disrespect me, but I have let go. I believe my work is done. You know right from wrong. I only wanted what's best for you, but I think you already know what's in your best interest. Please let me know what is it you want to do and good luck in all your endeavors.

Love always,
Mom

She did not cash the check, even when I signed it over to her because as my grandmother used to say and which so aptly applied to Candi, she knew on which side her bread was buttered.

> *Wednesday, April 15, 1998*
>
> *Two natures beat within my breast*
> *The one is foul, the one is blessed*
> *One I love, one I hate*
> *The one I feed, that one will dominate*
>
> Dr. David Jeremiah

Curfew

Since I didn't record a lot in her journal during her senior year, I can only explain a few significant issues that came up and how we dealt with them. Candi had two new best friends and she spent a lot a time with them. She hated that I referred to them as her two new best friends when they had been together since first grade. I called them that because their character had changed. They were always telling her that I was a fanatic and overly strict. The three took several classes together, and for the senior year, they were grouped together to complete their SIP (Senior Investigative Project).

I have come to believe that as graduation looms closer and with all the high expectations and excitement in the air, there is an adrenalin rush for most seniors. Many get a little carried away and Candi was no different. She was in the thick of things. She was riding high, knowing she would soon be going away and I would be out of her hair. In the meantime, she was just having a ball with her friends. She already had most of her high school credits and having a job and her very own car, she could not have desired anything else. If I didn't put my foot down, she would have only come home to sleep. Yes, I did understand that there were a lot of things going on in her life, but Candi always had to overdo everything.

I established a weekend curfew. She had to be home before midnight. Well, of course she had to test the limit. She would come home at 12:15, 12:25 etc. We argued a lot about this, so finally I put my foot down. I stood in the garage and waited for 12:00 on the dot and then I flipped the switch so that the automatic door opener wouldn't function. She came home at 12:03. She rang the doorbell repeatedly and pounded on the door. Of course, all this time I was standing right behind the door. I finally opened it up and confronted her. Needless to say, she was as mad as a wrongly shot hog. Regardless, I got my point across. She made it home before 12:00 every time after that.

By permission of Leigh Rubin and Creators Syndicate, Inc.

I just love it when I get these little confirmations. Even if it is a cartoon, someone else must be seeing it my way.
— Mom

Graduation

Well, what do you know? Graduation came and Candi finished high school on the high honor roll. She got excellent grades without putting out much effort, it seems to me. She was just gifted with a good aptitude for learning, so it came easily for her. Once she was able to filter out certain ideas, deal with her anger, and put things into perspective, she started getting the good grades that she was accustomed to receiving.

Garbage Incident

I still smile when I think about the following incident. One Thursday night in July, Candi asked me if she could spend the night with one of her two new best friends. I knew that the parents of that particular young lady were out of town. So, I told Candi she could not go since there would be no supervision. She tried to assure me that it would be just the three girls looking at the video from graduation. Even so, I still said no. Incredibly, Candi did not argue. At ten o'clock she kissed me good night and was most pleasant as she went downstairs to her bedroom. I felt so relieved that we didn't have a blow-out argument. I promptly went to sleep.

Now, garbage day was Friday and I would usually put the garbage out Thursday night. That particular Thursday I did not put out the recycle bins because there was very little in them. At 6:00 o'clock the next morning a voice woke me up, "Put out the recycle bins." My first thought was, *Forget it. There is hardly anything in them*, and I turned over to go back to sleep. Again the voice said, "Get up and put out the recycle bins." Again I dismissed it and turned over to get back to sleep. Well, the voice grew louder in my head, so I literally spoke out loud, "Ok! I will put out the recycle bins!" Truly, I wasn't thinking about the Ruach HaKodesh (Holy Spirit) at that moment.

I put my robe over my nightgown and walked downstairs. I opened the garage, picked up the almost empty blue and yellow bins, and headed down the driveway. Halfway to the street, I glanced to the left and lo and behold, there was Candi with one foot in the window trying to get in the den. I yelled at her, "Candi, what are you doing?" I took the bins to the end of the curb and came back inside. A very contrite and seemingly repentant child explained what had happened. Her two dear friends encouraged her to leave her car in the garage, climb through the window and they would wait for her at the end of the street. You see, she couldn't take her own car because I might have heard the garage door open and they couldn't risk that.

Honestly, I didn't really scold Candi. I asked her how she would have felt if she would have come back home to find yellow tape around the house and police cars everywhere. I then explained to her how the Lord loved us and how the Ruach HaKodesh (Holy Spirit) awakened me. She understood and so there was no need to prolong the discussion.

There were several incidents like that during the two years before Candi went to college. This particular one I feel was the most dramatic. Her friends had even tried to tell her several times that I was psychic. Obviously, they were seeing something noteworthy in our lives to have drawn such a conclusion.

Candi and I had several disagreements over the summer and I couldn't wait for the end of August to deposit her at the college. Incidentally, she went to a small Christian college. This decision came about with not too much disagreement. You see, I held the trump card. If she went to a secular college, she paid the tuition; if she went to a Christian college, I paid. There wasn't too much room for argument.

I also had the opportunity to choose the curfew time for Candi on the weekends, during her freshman year at the college. I signed that she had to be in by midnight. Talk about her anger when she later found out what I had done. She was incensed, but since she was hundreds of miles from me, the most she could do was hang up the phone on me, her mother. Another great rule at that college is that each student had a booklet which needed to be stamped confirming their attendance to sixteen Christian events per semester. Receiving their grades hinged on it.

Many Christian teenagers can go to secular colleges without having their relationship with Christ damaged in any way. My daughter was not one of them. I didn't feel like she was grounded enough to hold on to her faith in the midst of pressure and all sorts of negative influences. My God-given responsibility was to strengthen the foundation so that Candi would stand up for her faith in the midst of any kind of testing.

The last night before we left for Grove City College, I wrote Candi a last letter. Although it was late and I was tired, I felt that it was important to write my last little bit of encouragement.

Friday, August 28, 1998
11:05 P.M.

Dear Can,

It has been quite a long trek and an uphill battle, but God has always been at the helm. I write this little note with mixed feelings and emotions.

I know you have this misconceived idea that Mom is happy that you are leaving. I am happy, but you don't understand why. God directed you to the Christian College. He gave me an assignment which I have completed, but as long as we would have continued living as we have been for the past two years, I would have continued trying to do the work that God now has to do in a different setting, and without me. Remember our favorite Bible verse, Deuteronomy 6: 5-9? Read it again. I have planted the seed, but I haven't done a good job of letting God water it. Now that you are completely in His hands, you will either heed His call or suffer the consequences—which will be quite difficult and painful. Frankly, I am quite excited to sit back and see what our Father will do.

I am also exuberantly, ecstatically excited—jumping out of my skin with joy because you are not at a secular college. If you were, I would have been bawling my eyes out because I believe that Satan would have been having his field day. See, then you would have, mistakenly so, thought that I was crying because I missed you. Try to see the double irony in that situation.

Honey, I love you with all my heart. You need to grow and I believe you will. Remember "the effectual, fervent prayer of a righteous man avails much." Become a prayer warrior. Feed your soul and your mind with God's word and remember your good friends like Brian (smile), Leah, Maureen, Rachel, Ann, Candace, Kurt and all the others in your prayers. The hour is drawing nigh and what better joy than to have loved ones sharing eternity with us. Then there is always your dad.

Tonight before you go to sleep, read Matthew 10: 32-39. That was the reading God laid on my heart sometime last year. If you read this journal, you will find the entry.

Can, whenever you are down or feeling sad, pick up your Bible. I know you think that I am missing a few or many screws, but Candi, the Lord has INCREDIBLE ways of communicating with me and when you become in tuned to Him, you will hear Him. Candi, I am so excited for us. May God be your all in all, the Friend that sticks closer than a brother— our Abba (Dad) Father.

Be good, Honey. Take care and remember that at any time, you could just be sitting, standing, sleeping and in the twinkling of an eye—you will be home forever. Thank God that He gave you to me. It has been a difficult task, but if your name is written in Glory, I will have passed the only important test. Call me any time, Sweetheart.

All my love, in Christ
Mom

Earrings

Candi's rebellion didn't actually stop when she started college. She continued to challenge my authority. She asked me if she could get a third piercing on the cartilage in her ear. I told her no. Now, before someone asks, "What's the big deal?", my contention is to question why people do such things. Why do people get tattoos? Why do people have ten pairs of earrings in each ear? Why do people pierce their tongue, their eyelids or anything else for that matter? My concern is not the outward visual manifestation. I question the motive. Did Candi just want to challenge me to get her own way? I guess I will never know. I simply said no and that was that.

Well, in October Candi called home and in her very sweet, demure little voice she said she had a secret to tell me, and I had to promise I wouldn't get mad. I trapped myself. I responded that as long as she was still a virgin, there wasn't anything we couldn't deal with. Then she blurted out, "I pierced my ear."

My immediate response was, "You don't live here anymore." At first she tried to plead with me, but when her overtures fell on deaf ears, she got upset. Finally, she simply said fine and slammed the phone down. There was almost a month of silence between Candi and me. She never called or e-mailed and neither did I. The week before Thanksgiving, she called. In a very soft, low-keyed voice she said, "Hi, Mom."

"Hi Candi."

"May I come home for Thanksgiving?"

"Do you still have the third earring in your ear?"

"No, Mom."

"Ok, Honey. I'll see you in a few days.

For me, this event was significant and I felt it necessary to include it. Maybe it is food for thought for one of you, my readers. Each person has to know his or her child and deal with situations according to the leading of the Ruach HaKodesh (Holy Spirit). Today, as an adult, when she knows that I wouldn't have the right to object or interfere, Candi has not had any desire to pierce her ears. I stand by my decision.

Chapter Nine

NICE SURPRISES

Candi age 3

Here is a little note that Candi sent me when her great grandmother died. She referred to my grandmother as Gran because that's what everyone called her.

Oct. 2001

Mom,

How are you? I hope you are having a good week. I hope the plans for Gran's funeral are going smoothly. I am saddened because I was hoping to see Gran during my Christmas break. Well, I hope our family can at least come together and not argue about the arrangements for the funeral. I love you, Mom. I know God is very proud of you for the way you took care of Gran and for the way you brought me up. There is nothing more that you could've done. I just wanted to send you a quick note to tell you that I love you. Have a good week.

Love,
Your PPB. :)

A surprisingly nice, sweet change in attitude, wouldn't you say? Notice how she signed this note with PPB and a smile. I will explain this later.

Here is also one I sent her when I sent a little gift package as a surprise.

> **A GIFT FOR:**
> Name: Candi S. Bogues
> Campus Box # (if applicable): 1629
> Room #: 153
> Residence Hall: NORTH
> Campus Phone #: 458-2354
> Year of Graduation: 2002
> Item(s) You Are Ordering: The Fruit Basket
>
> *You may use the back of this card to write a personal message to your student.*

> Can
> God has been faithful.
> Philippians 4:19
> But my God shall supply all your need according to his riches in glory by Christ Jesus.
>
> He loves you before the foundation of this earth and so do I.
> In Him
> MOM

These little notes are only significant because they show that the lines of communication between Candi and me, though not perfect, had certainly come a long way.

I mailed the little cartoon on the next page to Candi while she was in college. These little things must have touched her because she kept them, for which I was pleasantly surprised. Frankly, that is how I found a lot of little articles. She actually kept adding little pieces of papers and notes to this journal. I guess as parents we have to realize that even when it seems like our children aren't listening, they are actually hiding things in their hearts. At least that is what I discovered with Candi, after the fact.

See Can, someone else feels like I do. I love you

As I told you, when Candi left for college, I gave her the journal you have been reading, that I had written to her while she was in high school. After she read it, she called me and said in a horrified, very apologetic tone of voice, "MOM! I wasn't that bad, was I?!!"

"No, Candi. You weren't that bad." I answered soothingly, then jokingly added, "You were worse! There is no vocabulary that could've described what you were really like."

There was a long pause. Then, suddenly, we both started laughing. Candi said jokingly, "Well, Mom, you were a pain, too."

"Well, you were a pain, pest, and bother," I retorted with a chuckle.

This was the turning point. The tension between us was finally broken. Since then, Candi always greets me with a cheerful, hearty, "Hi, Pain," and I answer back, "Hello, Pain, Pest, and Bother." To us, these are terms of endearment. They are born out of the bonding that came from going through that horrible time together. Candi even signs her letters, PPB, as you can see on page 110. If Candi calls me Mom, I know she is upset with me about something. If she uses "Pain," I know everything is okay.

Recently, I discovered a very nice surprise about those years. In the fall of 2007 I decided that I would sell our home in the spring. Candi was already married and long gone. I certainly didn't need all the extra room anymore. As I was cleaning out boxes and other things, I found Candi's agenda from her senior year. Out of curiosity I started thumbing through the pages and was shocked at what I found. There were little Bible verses that I must have written to her when I stopped recording in the journal. I couldn't remember even doing that. When I spoke to Candi, she confirmed that I would sometimes put a verse in her paper bag lunch. (A regular lunch box was not cool for a senior.)

Candi's remark to me was, "I bet you thought I never read them. Well, I did. I never threw any out."

Thank you, Honey.

I believe this validates what the Bible says: The Spirit intercedes *for us with groanings that cannot be uttered* (Romans 8:26 KJV). I believe the Ruach HaKodesh was interceding for Candi and me as He nudged me to write those little verses (which I wrote almost subconsciously, since I can't remember). Then He spoke to Candi through them.

I will end this chapter with these little verses. .

Defiant Daughter *Divine Grace*

SUNDAY 25 JANUARY

MONDAY JANUARY 26

TUESDAY JANUARY 27

– Phillippian 4:13
– I can do all things through Christ who strengthens me.

Love,
Mom

WEDNESDAY JANUARY 28

AP Calc BC 12:00
RM 151 152
bring pen + pencil

STUDY TIP: *Need to improve your language skills? Read often.*

THURSDAY JANUARY 29

Need journal Sheet

Priorities: Visa bill   21.06
                       135.47
         Total $156.53

FRIDAY JANUARY 30

Proverbs 22:3 A wise man sees danger a far off and flees from it, but the simple keeps going and suffer for it.

Priorities:

SATURDAY JANUARY

MEMO

1 John 2 15 & 17
  Do not love the world or anything in the world. If anyone loves the world, the love of the Father is not in him.
  The world and its desires pass away, but the man who does the will of God lives forever.

IMAGINE:
You pay $20 for ???ter. But the clerk over-charges you by $5. ?ishonest, ?ives you back and ?ckets $2. If you got ?ack, you paid $17. ?d to that the $2 the clerk ?ept, and e total is only $19.
Q. Where's the missing money?

Defiant Daughter *Divine Grace*

SUNDAY 1 FEBRUARY

MONDAY 2 FEBRUARY

Matthew 6:21 & 22 ♡♡
But store up for yourselves treasures in heaven, where moth and rust do not destroy, and where thieves do not break in and steal.
For where your treasure is, there your heart will be also.
♡ Mom

TUESDAY 3 FEBRUARY

Romans 1:16
I am not ashamed of the gospel because it is the power of God for the salvation of everyone who believes; first for the Jew, then for the Gentile.

WEDNESDAY 4 FEBRUARY

It's the longest tug-of-war ever: two groups of British soldiers pull for 161 minutes! 1889.

Proverbs 1:10   🎀 + 🎀 = God's love
      Candi Mom
My Son, if sinners entice you, do not give in to them.
     ♡♡ Love,
        Mom

STUDY TIP: Keep working! It's cliché but true: steady wins the race.

THURSDAY FEBRUARY 5

Priorities:

FRIDAY FEBRUARY 6

PIG - write a letter about something to someone (all the things you saw that were a result of public tak) analyze an article or issue
PAU, PP, PSI, PG.

Priorities:

SATURDAY 7 FEBRUARY

Nahum 1:7

The Lord is good, a refuge in times of trouble. He cares for those who trust in him.

hugs & kisses ♡♡♡

love always,
Mom

Defiant Daughter *Divine Grace*

SUNDAY 8 FEBRUARY

MONDAY 9 FEBRUARY

1 Corinthians 1:8 He will keep you strong to the end, so that you will be blameless on the day of our Lord Jesus Christ.
Amen. Love Mom

TUE FEB 10

Proverbs 18:24
There is a friend that sticketh closer than a brother.
Guess who?

Hebrews 10:12
If we deliberately keep on sinning after we have received the knowledge of the truth, no sacrifice for sin is left

WEDNESDAY 11 FEBRUARY
PIG - write five should statements

Job 23:10
When he hath tried me, I shall come forth as gold
Love

STUDY TIP: *Memorization isn't much fun. But it works!*

THURSDAY FEBRUARY 26

Romans 8:7
 The sinful mind is hostile to God. It does not submit to God's laws nor can it do so.

FRIDAY FEBRUARY 27

Romans 13:14 Rather, clothe yourselves with the Lord Jesus Christ and do not think about how to gratify the desires of the sinful nature.

Isaiah 29:5-6
 ...Suddenly in an instant the Lord Almighty will come with Thunder and earthquake and great noise...

Isaiah 26:3
 You will keep in perfect peace, him whose mind is steadfast because he trusts in you.

Proverbs 12:1
 Whoever loves discipline, loves knowledge, but he who hates correction is stupid.

Defiant Daughter Divine Grace

SUNDAY 1 MARCH

MONDAY MARCH 2

2 Corinthians 4:18 ... Fix your eyes not on what is seen, but on what is unseen. For what is seen is temporary, but what is unseen is eternal.

TUESDAY MARCH 3

Math - pg 703 #1-11 odd, 19, 23, 24, 25, 29, 30, 37

Hebrews 2:18 Because he himself suffered when he was tempted he is able to help those who are being tempted.

WEDNESDAY MARCH 4

It's a big year for humanity: we learn to write, 3100 B.C.

Math - pg. 713 # 1, 5, 7, 8, 9, 11, 15, 16, 17, 19

Lamentations 3:23. The Lord is good to those whose hope is in him; to those who seek him.

Nice Surprises   123

STUDY TIP: Ask your teacher how long you should spend preparing for a test.

THURSDAY MARCH 5

Priorities:

FRIDAY MARCH 6

Priorities: Jeremiah 17:5 ... Cursed is the one who trusts in man, who depends on flesh for his strength and whose heart turns away from the Lord.

SATURDAY

Say what you mean; mean what you say.

MEMO — Jeremiah 17:10 I, the Lord search the heart and examine the mind to reward a man according to his conduct, according to what his deeds deserve.

"She calls a spade a delving instrument." — RITA MAE BROWN

Defiant Daughter *Divine Grace*

SUNDAY 8 MARCH

MONDAY

3 John 1:11 Dear Friend, do not imitate what is evil, but what is good. Anyone who does what is good is from God. Anyone who does what is evil, has not seen God

TUESDAY MARCH 10

Math - 11.7 #1-25 odd in packet
English - read ditto and do questions.

WEDNESDAY MARCH 11

So that's how you spell it: the first dictionary is written, 20 B.C.

STUDY TIP: In class, don't forget to open your ears as well as your mouth!

THURSDAY MARCH 12

Romans 5:3 ... but we also rejoice in our sufferings because we know that suffering produces perseverance

FRIDAY MARCH 13

PIG - make questions for poll ♥

Math - pg 765 #19-30 and a ?

Jude v. 21
Keep yourselves in God's love as you wait for the mercy of our Lord Jesus Christ to bring you to eternal life

SATURDAY MARCH

2 Timothy 3:1-2 ... in the last days people will be lovers of themselves, lovers of money, boastful, proud, abusive, disobedient to their parents, ungrateful, unholy ...

2 John 8-9 Watch out that you do not lose what you have worked for, but that you may be rewarded fully. 9. Anyone who runs ahead and does not continue in the teaching of Christ, does not have God ...

Seen in a Tokyo hotel:
IS FORBIDDEN TO STEAL HOTEL towels please. If your are not a person to do such thing is please not to read notis.

"I may not know how to use 34 words where 3 would do, but that does not mean I don't know what I'm talking about."
— RUTH SHAYS

126 Defiant Daughter *Divine Grace*

SUNDAY 15 MARCH

MONDAY MARCH 16

Calculus: Study for test

PIG: write intro. paragraph to pig poll

AP BIOLOGY: Review notes, and read Daniel book.

Job 5:9 He performs wonders that cannot be fathomed, miracles that cannot be counted.

Mon. March 16, 1998

TUES. MARCH 17 — St. Patrick's Day

Isaiah 30:15... In repentance and rest is your salvation, in quietness and trust is your strength.

Tues. March 17, 1998

Priorities:

WEDNESDAY MARCH 18 — The average English speaker has a vocabulary of 4000 words, 1997.

Jack Astor's

~~Math pg. 741 #1-13odd~~

Psalm 25:3 No one whose hope is in you will ever be put to shame, but he will be put to shame who are treacherous without excuse.

Priorities:

As one of my most victorious moments and a wonderful surprise, Candi finally made the decision to be baptized after she graduated from college. She was baptized in November of 2002. It was for me pure joy. She did it on her own when she was good and ready. I believe that the influence of her church as well as her college experience did a lot to mature her walk with Christ.

Chapter Ten

CANDI AS AN ADULT

Candi's college graduation

Candi is now a physician assistant (PA) at one of our local hospitals, working mostly in surgery. This is a great achievement for her, but getting there wasn't easy. I guess I could say that she fumbled around a bit as she tried to identify the path that the Lord wanted her to follow.

First, she did a summer in-service at the local medical examiner's office. The highlight of that summer was the opportunity to dissect a decomposing body to figure out the cause of death. Soon she was gung-ho about becoming a pathologist. But when she found out how much schooling it would take, her enthusiasm dampened. Later, she realized that each county hires only one medical examiner. She said to me, "Mom, how would I get a job? There wouldn't be any opening for me until the current examiner died!"

She then explored the idea of becoming a pharmaceutical representative because one of her friends working as one, really enjoyed it. Well, that idea soon fell by the wayside. She spent another summer doing an internship in Texas for her lab research class, studying rat cells. She enjoyed that so much that she wanted to become a geneticist or some type of lab researcher. But after one year she told me, "I don't want to spend the rest of my life working in a lab where I will never be around people!" So, that idea was also scrapped. Subsequently, she began taking courses to become a pharmacist, but it also did not work out.

In the end, Candi graduated from college with a bachelor's degree in biochemistry and came home with no idea what her next move would be. She started slipping into the defiant role that she was so used to playing and seemed to have mastered so well. I was not about to revisit that era, so I made it quite plain that people with a biochemistry degree go back to college and choose a career path. She thought of becoming a surgeon, but couldn't deal with the many years of study it would take. So, she did nothing.

To ensure that Candi and I did not revert back into our old roles, I picked up an application at the local pharmacy for a pharmacy technician. She got the job and started taking some graduate courses at the local university. It was then that she decided to become a physician's assistant with the goal of working in surgery. She worked very hard in her studies and ended up with a GPA of 3.78, much improved from her undergraduate 2.7 GPA. For her last year of graduate school she got a 4.0!

Today, Candi is a surgical PA who is very enthusiastic about her job. She is very disciplined and hardworking, enjoys the interaction with her patients, and working collegially and cooperatively with the different surgeons. She finds it fulfilling and rewarding to be able to actively participate in the surgeries, pray for her patients and sit back and watch the healing take place. She has been often encouraged to become a doctor, and has given it serious thoughts, but is reluctant to put in all the years of study and commitment that would entail. I often remind her that our Father is still able to use her in a powerful way, wherever she labors or serves.

Candi is well-loved by all our neighbors and friends. They have watched her grow up and they do feel a big part of her life. It warms my heart to listen to all their compliments as to how wonderful she is today. I chuckle inside as I think to myself, "If only the half had been told." Many seem to think that she is the best thing since sliced bread. Oh, what a marvelous Father to have done such an incredible job with the piece of defective pottery that He had.

My hopes and dreams are that Candi will always put God first in every aspect of her life, without compromise; and that from her own experience and observation, she will be able to realize that it is only what we do for Christ that will truly last. I am happy to say that she already expresses this belief and determination. Should Candi ever become a parent, I hope she will also be able to instill this into her children.

Candi's Perspective

In July 2009 my editor asked Candi the following questions.

How do you see those years from your perspective? What was going on in your head back then?

I believe I was angry at the situation of my parents' divorce and angry at my father. I never had a real relationship with my dad nor have I ever had a true heart-to-heart talk with him. When we go visit him today, my husband notices that my father hardly looks at me and doesn't say much to me.

There was no yelling or arguing with my dad. It may have been from fear of him, but I never experienced any wrath from him from my talking back. Even now I can only count a handful of times that I stood up to him and that was over the phone, knowing that whatever wrath he might have, couldn't be so bad from miles away. The divorce was the best thing for my parents, yet the end result caused many arguments between my mom and me.

How did you see the earring incident?

I thought my mom was being difficult and unfair. The earring was so tiny. It could barely be seen when I had my hair down. I still remember her threat when I told her about the earring. Her response was, "Get rid of the earring or don't bother coming home for Thanksgiving." I thought that was ridiculous. Well, my mother had a way of still scaring you even when you were many miles away at college. I remember quickly trying to remove the earring from my ear in the driveway after being dropped off from college by a friend who drove me home for the holidays.

I even saved the earring and tried later that night to replace it in my ear. Needless to say, I believe God made sure that hole closed up quickly because for the life of me, I could not get the stupid thing back in my ear. I was truly surprised considering that the earring had been in my ear for a whole month and there is no reason why it shouldn't go back easily in the hole. Looking back, I truly believe it was the Lord showing me that He agreed with my mother's stance on the issue. I also believe that nothing that I could have tried would have opened back up that hole. That was ten years ago. My husband now is even happy that I only have one hole in each ear and I have to admit that today I don't even want put a third earring in my ear.

How did it make you feel to attend Grove City College as opposed to the secular Universty?

At first I was upset. I saw the University as a big school with many more opportunities. Grove City College is set in a small town with a population for the minority at two percent. Once at Grove City, I realized I liked the small size school and the smaller classrooms. My professors actually knew my name and still remember me many years after graduating. I was even able to do lab work on the side for my biology and chemistry professors.

There were still times that I wished I could have experienced a larger school setting, but looking back now, I see that the smaller school setting and the one-on-one time with professors were invaluable.

How do you see your mom now? What did she do right and why was it right for you?

My mom was a strong person back then for doing what she had to do and I still believe she is a strong person now. The only way that it was possible is through Christ. I know she prayed for me every night because she loved me. That's not to say that she liked me very much through the years of 1996 to 2004.

I know my mom was strict and I may not have been able to do as many things as other kids in school, but I stayed on the straight and narrow path. I have made some mistakes in my life, but that is a far cry from what I could have done had it not been for the strict mother I had who stood her ground.

What would your advice be to the parent of a difficult child?

Stand your ground. When you make a decision whether or not you feel it is right, be firm. Wavering from a decision you make will let your child see you as a pushover. I have seen this with other people and their parents while I was growing up, and I still see it now as an adult. I have not had children yet, but I hope I can do the same as my mother did, even though at times I know it must have been difficult for her to feel like the bad guy all the time. Parents out there, your children may not appreciate your decision today or even tomorrow, but one day they will have kids and be in the same situation and will realize that there are not always easy ways to discipline and raise a child.

Chapter Eleven

THE LORD IS GOOD

Candi's senior portrait

One of the questions that many people are curious about and often ask is how I managed financially after the divorce. My only response really is that God is incredible. In Genesis 22:14 (KJV) it states: *"And Abraham called the name of that place Jehovah Jireh"* (which means *"the Lord will provide"*).

Wherever the Lord leads He provides. I must address the issue of divorce here. God says that he hates divorce and I struggled with that when it became a reality that this was the finality of my marriage. I fasted and prayed a lot. The Lord directed me to 2 Corinthians 6: 14-18. Please read it before continuing and ask the Lord to open your understanding. It is the only way to accept the information in this little book as coming from the Lord. I had stepped out of God's perfect will, but in His grace and mercy, He gave me His permissive will.

Together my husband I were making over a six figure salary. I still recall the money issues we often argued about. When he left, he took two-thirds of the matrimonial income. Was I concerned about financial issues? Of course I was. If we had difficulty making ends meet with an income over a hundred thousand, how would I make it on one-third of that?

All the literature out there will tell you that single parents are the new American poor. Our God is a God of miracles. He says that you will never see *"the righteous forsaken nor his seed begging bread"* (Psalm 37:25 KJV). I stepped out in faith. I cut back on several things and made a budget, which, by the way, never did seem to come out right. My savings was practically depleted because I had bought my husband's share of the house. I didn't think it was fair to Candi to have to endure too many changes all at the same time. Staying in our home was something I decided was necessary and important. Looking back now, I think I was right. It would have been devastating for her if we would have had to move.

In all the years that I have walked with the Lord, I have never prayed more than I did during that period after the divorce. I reminded the Lord that He promised to provide for all my needs. I quoted back several of His promises to Him. When I would get upset, stressed out, or unsure, I would open my Bible, point to a promise, and out loud remind the Lord what He said. For example, Psalm 27:10 (KJV), *"When my mother and father forsake me, then the Lord will take me up."* I would point to those words and to others and tell the Lord, "You promised to be a Father to the fatherless." I treated the Lord as a Father. I trusted Him to keep His word and I reminded Him of it almost daily. I don't want to belabor the point. Suffice it to say that if God were a human being, He would have started running every time He saw me coming. I knocked at His door twenty-four hours a day, every day, and I always came armed with the Scriptures.

Now, back to financial matters. I was a tithing Christian. I knew that there was no way I could rob the Lord. I knew Malachi 3:10–11 by heart, and I knew there was a consequence for disobeying it. I also knew that the Lord would have to keep His end of it, and He did.

The court did require Candi's dad to pay child support which he did. He had tried to get out of it, but my attorney had informed him in a rather terse letter that he'd better pay up or my attorney would personally bring litigation against him. Henceforth, there was never any issue with his adhering to his responsibility. It was also stated that he was responsible for paying two-thirds of Candi's tuition for college, and I would pay the other third which worked out well.

I am a good steward of God's blessings. I spend my money carefully and I usually save for big ticket items. I use my credit card(s) but always with the understanding that whatever I charge, I pay off at the end of the month. I NEVER carry a balance. If I don't think I will be able to pay off the full amount at the end of the month, then I don't make that purchase. That is also a concept that I have taught Candi which, thank the Lord, she practices to this day.

My husband moved out on September the fifth and in October a friend approached me and asked if I would be willing to help out a sister in Christ. This sister, let's call her Reva, was planning to move to Florida within a two to three months and needed somewhere to stay. She couldn't afford much rent, but asked if I would agree for her to stay with me for a contribution of one hundred and fifty dollars a month to help out a little. I met with Reva and we talked. I explained to her that the Lord ruled in my home and as long as she was willing to put God first, I didn't see why we couldn't live together harmoniously for two to three months. She stayed with me for almost two years. She left only because my mother had that terrible auto accident in September of 2007 and moved in with me in April of 2008. This was just one of the many ways the Lord provided for me!

I can't put a finger on precisely how I managed financially. The Lord just took care of everything. Not only did I have abundance, but in 2005, I was able to pay off the mortgage on our home. My mother gave Candi two thousand dollars toward purchasing a car which helped me to get her a decent little car for $5,500. Then of course, good old Candi, the forever complainer, griped about the car. So when she left for college, I sold it and bought her a brand new 1999 Honda Civic. Then, of course, when she slid into the ditch one miserable winter day in December of 1999, she complained that it was because the Civic was too light and didn't stay put on the road. Of course, there was a winter storm warning in effect with the public being advised not to do any unnecessary travel. Candi knew about the winter advisory, but chose to drive to the next city nonetheless.

Nevertheless, later I drove the car and really didn't like the handling on the road. So I prayed, sought the Lord, and I traded in the Civic and got her a 2001 Honda Accord. The Lord provided the funds to purchase all these automobiles for cash. My only explanation again is God provides. Even when we whine, moan, groan, and complain like Candi seemed to have had a propensity to do, He still has the heart of a loving Father.

Something that occurred in 1999 really tested my faith. My oldest sister in Jamaica and I took care of our paternal grandmother. She provided housing and I would send some money to help out with food. I gave my sister sixty dollars per month which was a rather small amount, but we agreed that this would be fine. Well, my grandmother was getting older and less capable, and my sister didn't want the actual burden any more. A good Christian friend agreed that my grandmother could stay with her and I would give her three hundred dollars monthly. I went racing to the Lord, very agitated and out of my mind with dismay. "Where pray tell do You expect me to come up with this king's ransom to pay for Gran's upkeep?!" I can still hear myself saying this to the Lord.

Later, I more calmly said, "Ok, Lord, I can afford the first three hundred, but Gran is your child too. The same promises that you have given to me, are relevant for her also. If you provide the three hundred dollars, after this initial payment, I will gladly send it for Gran's upkeep."

The Lord provided that three hundred dollars every single month. Gran passed away in September of 2001 at the age of ninety-two. Never once in all that time did I stress out about the three hundred dollars. It was always readily available and right on time.

There is no magic formula that I or anyone else can present with regards to our survival in difficult and trying situations. Titus 1:2 says that God cannot lie. I took Him literally at His word and trusted Him to provide for me and Candi, and He did.

Proverbs 3:5-6 (KJV) says, *"Trust in the Lord with all thine heart and lean not unto thine own understanding. In all thy ways acknowledge Him and He shall direct thy paths."* We can learn a great lesson from the Children of Israel who wandered in the desert for forty years. The generation that witnessed all of God's miracles, but still doubted Him, did not enter the Promised Land. We cannot hold God in contempt and still expect to receive His best.

In the parable of the boy with the evil spirit in Mark 9: 17-24, the father asked the Lord to help his unbelief. He admitted that he knew Christ could heal his son, but at the point where he doubted, he asked the Lord to build his faith. We too must ask the Lord each day to build and increase our faith. Our walk with Christ needs renewing daily. I sought help in His word for physical and emotional support every day, as well as help to resolve financial issues, and He came through for me one hundred percent of the time.

Final Reflections

The idea first came to me to write this memoir because several of my friends who have a personal relationship with Yeshua (Jesus), especially a few single parents, wanted to know how I managed when I was thrust into this situation. [I say it again. In no way do I want this journal to be promoting single parenting. It is NOT God's ideal. He made Adam and Eve, the first parents, a male and a female. I believe that is the model He desires for us.]

Many people have asked to borrow Candi's journal and I was not averse to lending it, but like anything else, you lend it and you have a good chance of losing it. I thought if I could put everything together in book form, they could use it and, hopefully, glean a little of God's heart from it.

I do hope the people who have asked me to share Candi's journal will find it beneficial. I would like for others to not judge me too harshly. I am not perfect, but I believe that my Father has been able to use me mightily in my daughter's eyes. My only advice to parents is that I believe we are supposed to be Yeshua (Jesus) in our children's eyes. I hope I did that for my own child

What I really hope is that this journal has been a help to any of you parents reading it who are dealing with a difficult child. I hope it has been an encouragement to you to stay the course knowing that the Lord is with you and that there is a light at the end of the tunnel. Your Godly parenting will be rewarded.

I also hope that this journal will encourage all of God's children to reflect on His great and abiding love and strive, through His strength, to become more like Him each day.

This song succinctly summarizes what I believe God's desire is for us:

> Lord prepare me to be a sanctuary,
> Pure and holy, tried and true.
> With thanksgiving, I'll be a living
> Sanctuary for you.

Thompson and Scruggs © 1982 Whole Armor Publishing Co. CCLI #2410

* * *

In hindsight, I don't know if I would have done anything differently than I have done. The lessons that I have learned reach far beyond Candi. During the time that I was putting this journal together to make this book, I realized again how much I need the Lord and how much I learned back then to trust Him—to rely and depend on Him. As I reread the words that I wrote more than ten years ago, my spirit and my resolve are renewed. I pray that the Lord will continue to strengthen me so that I will never take my eyes off Him. I am amazed at how much He has loved me.

This journal has been a great help and reminder for me over the years because at times when I tend to become stressed, worried or doubtful, I go back and reflect on how faithful my Father was for me at a time when life was a bit too much for me to cope. As I read over the entries I am often overwhelmed and overcome with gratitude as to how miraculously things transpired for me. Then I reflect on these commands and promises that the Lord gives us in Joshua 1 5-9:

1) I will not fail thee, nor forsake thee
2). Be strong and very courageous
3). Be careful to obey all the law that you may prosper wherever you go
4). The Lord is with you wherever you go

Has this been the only time that God stood by me? Absolutely and most resoundingly not! This phase, however, was truly the start of a deeper intimacy and closeness with Christ. In order not to forget, or whenever fear or doubt attempt to overcome me, I always go back to that time and place when my Father met me, comforted me, guided me patiently, listened to me, and heard my every cry.

Like in Jeremiah 18, I was a marred piece of clay, so He took me down to the Potter's house and made a new vessel. It took me awhile to submit but, like the old adage, it's better late than never. This vessel is still a work in progress, but when I take a look at the woman in the mirror, I like what I see and to think, He is still not finished with me as yet. I can't wait to see where He will take me from here.

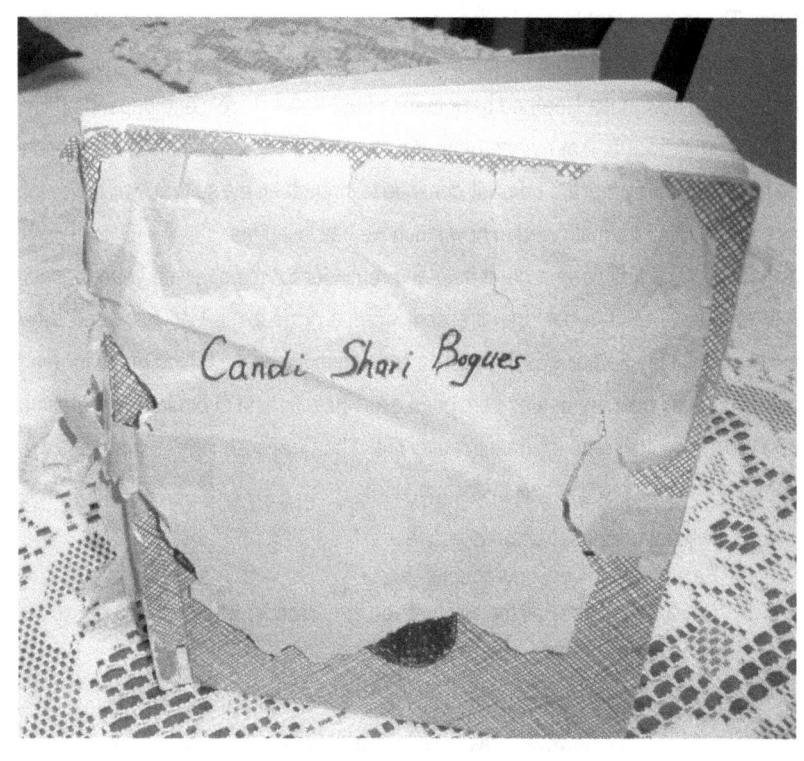

The lovingly written, gratefully read journal, now tattered and torn from being shared with so many interested friends.

About the Author

Lorna Bogues is a cheerful, loving person who declares the praises of Yeshua (Jesus) to everyone she knows. She has led many colleagues and friends to the Lord, of whom some are now leading others. She discovered the Messianic Movement in 2007 and promptly  joined a Judaism class to become a member of a Messianic congregation.

Lorna was a teacher in Jamaica and after completing her college credentials, she became a bilingual teacher here in the United States. She teaches at the middle grades and has had several different assignments over the years. She has taught Spanish, English, special education as well as some  academic intervention classes. She has done academic evaluations as part of the standardized testing for the district. Most recently she has been asked to become a teacher coordinator of special education. She resides with Mollie, a handicapped individual for whom she has guardianship.

This book is available at
olivepresspublisher.org
amazon.com
barnesandnobles.com
and more.

www.ingramcontent.com/pod-product-compliance
Lightning Source LLC
Chambersburg PA
CBHW071659040426
42446CB00011B/1837